CONTENTS

ABOUT THIS BOOK

This *Step by Step Guide* has been produced by the editors of Insight Guides, whose books have set the standard for visual travel guides since 1970. With top-quality photography and authoritative recommendations, this guidebook brings you the very best of New England in a series of 16 tailor-made tours.

WALKS AND TOURS

The tours in the book provide something to suit all budgets, tastes, and trip lengths. They begin in with walks in Boston and neighboring Cambridge, the most likely access point for the vast majority of visitors. Proceeding in a roughly clockwise direction, they cover selected highlights from all six states of New England.

The tours embrace a range of interests, so whether you are fascinated by Revolutionary history, planning to hike in national parks and forests, keen to gorge on clam chowder and lobster, or have kids to entertain, you will find an option to suit.

We recommend reading the whole of a tour before setting out. This should help you to familiarize yourself with the route and

Above: view of Boston's historic North End district; lighthouse near Portland, Maine; fall in the Berkshires, Massachusetts; Harvard University in Cambridge; the *Mayflower II* in Portsmouth, a replica of the ship that brought the Pilgrim Fathers to America.

to plan where to stop for refreshments – options for this are shown in the 'Food and Drink' boxes, recognizable by the knife-and-fork sign, on most pages.

For our pick of the walks by theme, consult Recommended Tours For… *(see pp.6–7).*

OVERVIEW

The tours are set in context by this introductory section, giving an overview of the region to set the scene, plus background information on food and drink, shopping, sports and outdoor activities, and entertainment. A succinct history timeline highlights the key events that have shaped New England.

DIRECTORY

Also supporting the tours is a Directory chapter, comprising a clearly organized A–Z of practical information, our pick of where to stay in the region, and select restaurant listings; these eateries complement the more low-key cafés and restaurants that feature within the tours and are intended to offer a wider choice for evening dining. Also included here are some nightlife listings.

The Authors

Award-winning travel writer and photographer Simon Richmond has authored the Step by Step guides to Boston and Tokyo, as well as writing and contributing to over 30 different travel guidebooks, from Cape Town to the Trans-Siberian Railway, for other publishers. Having lived in the UK, Japan, and Australia, he now lives in Boston and uses it as a base for exploring the diverse and beautiful New England region.

A number of the tours in this book were originally conceived by New England experts Bill and Kay Scheller.

INSIGHT GUIDES
NEW ENGLAND
Step by Step

700036759736

APA PUBLICATIONS
Part of the Langenscheidt Publishing Group

Margin Tips
Shopping tips, historical facts, handy hints and information on activities help visitors to make the most of their time in New England.

Feature Boxes
Notable topics are highlighted in these special boxes.

Key Facts Box
This box gives details of the distance covered on the tour, plus an estimate of how long it should take. It also states where the route starts and finishes, and gives key travel information such as which days are best to do the route or handy transport tips.

Route Map
Detailed cartography shows the tour clearly plotted with numbered dots. For more detailed mapping, see the pull-out map slotted inside the back cover.

Food and Drink
Recommendations of where to stop for refreshment are given in these boxes. The numbers prior to each restaurant/café name link to references in the main text. Restaurants in the Food and Drink boxes are plotted on the maps.

The $ signs at the end of each entry reflect the approximate cost of a three-course dinner for one, excluding beverages, tax, and tip. These should be seen as a guide only. Price ranges, also quoted on the inside back flap for easy reference, are:

Footers
Look here for the tour name, a map reference, and the main attraction on the double-page.

$$$$	over $60
$$$	$40–60
$$	$20–40
$	below $20

ACTIVITIES

Climb New England's highest peak, Mount Washington, just one of the many hikes threading through the White Mountains (tour 13); in winter, head there and to Vermont's Killington (tour 10) for skiing.

RECOMMENDED TOURS FOR...

ARCHITECTURE

Visit Providence (walk 7) and Newport (walk 8) to see grand civic buildings and the 'cottages' of 19th-century tycoons. For modern architecture see the Frank Gehry-designed Ray and Maria Stata Center at MIT (walk 2).

CHILDREN

Billings Farm (tour 10) and Shelburne Farms (tour 11) let kids interact with farmyard animals. New Hampshire's Lakes Region (tour 12) and White Mountains (tour 13) serve up game arcades, train rides, and theme parks.

ART FANS

The art collections of Harvard (walk 2), Yale (tour 9), and the Rhode Island School of Design (walk 7) are all excellent. In the Berkshires (tour 6), don't miss MASS MoCA and the Norman Rockwell Museum.

NATIONAL PARKS

For lush landscapes that burst into a myriad of autumn colours, Vermont (tours 10 and 11) is justly famous, as are the Berkshires (tour 6). Maine's Acadia National Park (tour 16) is well worth the trip Down East.

GARDEN LOVERS

Portsmouth's Strawbery Banke Museum (walk 14) has small-scale colonial-style gardens, while the grounds of mansions in Newport (walk 8) and the Berkshires (tour 6) offer up grand horticultural visions.

HISTORY BUFFS

Acquaint yourself with the Revolutionary sites on Boston's Freedom Trail (walk 1) and the route between Lexington and Concord (tour 3). Salem's Peabody Essex Museum (tour 4) should also be on your visit list.

FOOD AND DRINK

Boston (walk 1) is just one of New England's great culinary destinations; foodies should make reservations in Portland (tour 15) and Portsmouth (walk 14). And Cape Cod (tour 5) is great for seafood.

SHOPPERS

The outlet stores of Freeport (tour 15) will please bargain hunters. Snap up a book or collegiate T-shirt in Harvard (walk 2) or Yale (tour 9), or Red Sox memorabilia in Boston (walk 1).

WATER VIEWS

Take a ferry to Provincetown (tour 5), follow Newport's Cliff Walk (walk 8), sail to the Thimble Islands (tour 9), drive through the Lakes Region (tour 12), or cycle alongside Lake Champlain (tour 11).

OVERVIEW

An overview of New England's geography, character, and culture, plus illuminating background information on food and drink, shopping, sports and outdoor activities, entertainment, and history.

INTRODUCTION

Six states – Connecticut, Maine, Massachusetts, New Hampshire, Rhode Island, and Vermont – make up New England, a historic playground of sophisticated cities, bucolic villages, seaside resorts, and beautiful countryside.

Before You Go
For more travel information on New England, go to www. visitnewengland.com, or check out the tourism websites of each of the states *(see pp.102–3).*

In the northeast corner of the USA, sandwiched between Canada, New York State, and the Atlantic Ocean, lies New England, home of some of the oldest American archetypes: the white church steeple presiding over a tidy village green, the self-sufficient farmstead, the swimming hole beneath a covered bridge, the salt-sprayed fishing village tucked against a rock-bound coast.

These were just everyday sights for New Englanders until 19th-century Currier & Ives prints and 20th-century Norman Rockwell illustrations introduced them to people who had never set foot in the region. Despite the passage of time, they still exist today and provide a picturesque backdrop for the mixture of walks and driving tours in this guide.

HISTORY

Native Name
The Massachusetts Bay Colony was named after the native peoples of the area, the Massachusetts, which roughly translates as 'near the big hill'.

As you travel throughout the region's six states, there is plenty to remind you of why it is called New England. Many of the town and city names were adopted from across the Atlantic by 17th-century British settlers. It is here that you will find some of America's oldest and most illustrious seats of learning –

Harvard, Yale, and Brown – all with campuses modeled on old English universities. Even after political ties with Britain had been broken, ideas from the Old World – such as the abolition of slavery and the technology of the Industrial Revolution – found fertile ground here in the 19th century, bringing New England great wealth.

The coming of the railroads also stoked a fledgling tourism industry along the coast and in the mountains, where the wealthy built palatial summer homes and grand hotels. After World War II, tourism in New England became diffused and democratized, especially when entrepreneurs began stringing rope tows, and later chair lifts, along the sides of mountains that were destined to become ski resorts. National parks and state forests were set up to protect the most precious pieces of the environment for all to enjoy.

CLIMATE

New England has four distinct seasons. The first snow generally falls in November and continues intermittently through March. Spring, which can be fleeting, starts in April and is

characterized by crisp, clear days and chilly evenings. June to September can be very hot and humid, starting in July, although most of the season is pleasant due to the ocean breeze. Fall is glorious, and the famous New England multi-colored foliage peaks in mid-October as the temperature starts to plummet.

GETTING AROUND THE STATES

This guide zones in on specially selected key attractions in each state and organizes the suggested itineraries – none lasting more than three days – accordingly. The tours start with walks in Boston and neighboring Cambridge, the most likely access point for the vast majority of visitors. Proceeding in a roughly clockwise direction from Boston, several, if not all, of the routes can be linked up, time permitting, to enable visitors to construct anything from a long weekend in one state to a full month's vacation throughout all of New England. The Points to Note box at the start of each tour gives details on how to link with other routes.

Cradle of Liberty

Massachusetts (www.mass.gov), the most populous of the New England sextet, is known as the Cradle of Liberty; it was here that the War of Independence kicked off in 1775. The state continues to live up to its history of liberalism and free thought; this was the first state in the US to legalize same-sex marriages.

There are 183 National Historic Landmarks in Massachusetts. You can view many of these in Boston – the most European of American cities – on day trips to Lexington and Concord *(tour 3)* and out to Salem and Cape Ann *(tour 4)*, where the trappings of the wealth that flooded into the region in the subsequent centuries can be assessed.

Going farther back, the days of the Pilgrim Fathers can be experienced on a trip down Massachusetts's South Shore and out to the hooked tip of Cape Cod *(tour 5)*, dotted with picturesque villages and sweeping ocean vistas. Continue to follow in the footsteps of those earlier adventurers by heading inland to explore Pioneer Valley and the verdant Berkshire Hills *(tour 6)*.

Above from far left: the remote, seaswept coast of Maine; vibrant fall colors.

Below: Boston is the region's main hub.

Above from left: covered bridge in Vermont; Lake Champlain along Burlington's Waterfront Park; Federal-style architecture in Massachusetts.

The Ocean State

Neighboring Massachusetts to the south is Rhode Island (www.ri.gov). Growing out of the Providence Plantations colony established in 1636 by Roger Williams, a clergyman disillusioned with Massachusetts Bay's theocratic government, the diminutive state was the first of the 13 colonies to cut its ties with Britain.

Rhode Islanders are seldom more than 30 minutes' drive from the water in the Ocean State. Riverside Providence *(walk 7)*, the state capital, has recently emerged from the shadow of Boston as one of New England's most interesting and design-driven cities. Down the coast, chichi Newport *(walk 8)* continues to be a summer haven for the rich, although these days, for the price of admission, anyone is free to traipse through the town's jaw-dropping collection of 19th-century mansions.

The Constitution State

Taking its name from a Mohegan (a Native American tribe) word meaning 'place of the long tidal river', Connecticut's proximity to New York often means it gets overlooked as a part of New England. However, Connecticut (www.ct.gov) is home to the nation's oldest continuously published newspaper, the *Hartford Courant*, just one of many reminders of the state's long history of European settlement.

The state is bisected by the mighty Connecticut River, while its south edge raggedly borders the Long Island Sound. Along the latter you will find the kitsch maritime shops of Mystic, the naval base of New London, and the academic haunts of New Haven *(tour 9)*.

Mountains and Forests

It is in the next two states that the natural beauty of New England really starts to come to the fore. Sparsely populated Vermont (www.vermont.gov) may be landlocked, but it is notable for vast Lake Champlain

---

A Literary Tradition

One the best ways to gain an insight into the New England frame of mind is to read a book by one of its native writers. In the 19th century, authors centered in Boston and Concord created the first important movement in American literature. In 1836 Ralph Waldo Emerson published his philosophical essay *Nature*, while in the following years Emerson's neighbor, Henry David Thoreau, chronicled his relationship with the natural world and his sojourn in a hand-built cabin on the shores of Walden Pond (see p.46).

Nathaniel Hawthorne brought a psychological dimension to the American novel, casting a sharp eye on Puritan New England in *The Scarlet Letter* (1850). Hawthorne's friend Herman Melville used his knowledge of the New Bedford whaling industry as background for *Moby-Dick* (1851).

Adding further luster to New England's literary reputation in the mid-19th century were Louisa May Alcott (also a Concord resident), Henry Wadsworth Longfellow (whose home is preserved in Harvard, see p.42), and Mark Twain, who settled in Hartford, Connecticut. Toward the end of the century the Pulitzer Prize-winning author Edith Wharton took up residence in a grand house in Lenox (see p.62).

running down half of the state's west border. Overlooking the lake is Vermont's largest city, Burlington *(tour 11)*, one of the most laid-back of New England's urban centers. To get there, you will pass through the lush Green Mountains *(tour 10)*, starting in the arty town of Brattleboro and heading towards peaks that are home to some of New England's top ski resorts.

The modern history of New Hampshire (www.nh.gov) is almost as old as that of Massachusetts, with the first English settlements in Portsmouth *(walk 14)* dating back to 1623. You will begin to understand why it is known as the Granite State when you head inland to tour the magnificent White Mountains *(tour 13)*, rugged peaks that rise up over 3,000ft (915m). At the foot of the mountains lies the equally majestic Lakes Region *(tour 12)*.

North by Down East
Last, but by no means least, there is Maine (www.maine.gov), the largest of the New England states. Many visitors barely scratch the surface of what the Pine Tree State has to offer, sticking mainly to the 60-mile (96km) stretch of coast south of Portland. Here the towns of York, Ogunquit, Wells, and Kennebunkport all enjoy fine beaches.

But it is north of Portland *(tour 15)* that Maine's character asserts itself most clearly, along the ragged coastline to the far-flung Down East redoubts of Bar Harbor and Acadia National Park *(tour 16)*. With more time on your hands, you could really go off the beaten track to some of the unspoiled islands that flake off from the shoreline like thousands of rocky, pine-tree-clad crumbs.

POPULATION

Around 14.23 million people live in New England, about three quarters of them based in and around the biggest cities, such as Boston, Providence, and Hartford, in the southern states of Massachusetts, Rhode Island, and Connecticut, respectively. This leaves much of the rest of the region with a low population density and a traditional rural character and attitude in sharp contrast to the more multicultural urban centers toward the coast.

POLITICS AND ECONOMICS

Long known for its liberalism, New England is the heartland of the Democratic Party. However, three of the region's states (Connecticut, Vermont, and Rhode Island) have Republican governors. As in the past, New England's prime industries revolve around specialized foods (the region is famous for its lobsters, cranberries, and maple syrup) and manufacturing, particularly electronic equipment. While this last sector has taken a hit during the latest economic downturn, the region's tourism industry remains buoyant.

Packed Population
The smallest of the New England states, Rhode Island is also one of the most densely populated, with just over 1 million people crammed into 1,545 sq miles (4,002 sq km).

FOOD AND DRINK

While proudly aware of its traditionalist roots, 'New England cuisine' is no longer the contradiction in terms it once was – you will now find some of America's best chefs making delicious creations from top-grade local produce.

The culinary tradition of New England synthesizes old English cookery techniques with the ingredients that were available to the colonies. A dish such as New England boiled dinner – beef brisket poached with root vegetables and cabbage – might easily have graced an English table 300 years ago. In terms of local additions, early New Englanders could dip into an immense natural larder bursting with game, fish and shellfish, native berries, and that great gift of the Indians, corn (maize).

Why Beantown?
Back in the 18th century, the city of Boston was awash with molasses shipped in from the Caribbean as part of the rum trade. This was mixed with salt pork and beans to make baked beans, once the quint-essential Boston dish – hence the city's nickname, Beantown. These days baked beans are not a common menu item; if you fancy trying them head to Union Oyster House (see p.32).

TRADITIONAL STANDBYS

Today's visitors to the region will have no trouble finding old standbys, such as Yankee pot roast (similar to the boiled dinner, but made with prime roast beef and a thickened gravy), creamy clam or fish chowder, and Indian pudding. The latter, a baked corn porridge affair, is usually served – as it definitely wasn't during colonial times – with vanilla ice cream. But these time-honored dishes have largely been relegated to the menus of restaurants that make a specialty of them, and of 'ye olde' colonial decor too.

New England has long since joined the trend toward a cuisine greatly influenced by new European and Asian concepts of super-fresh ingredients, lighter stocks and sauces, and a contrast of flavors and textures. There is, moreover, the element of authentic ethnic dining; most cities and college towns offer a broad range of world cuisines – none more so than Boston.

ETHNIC AND TRENDY

The diverse immigrant population of New England's principal city has bequeathed it a fine range of ethnic

restaurants. Chinatown is primarily packed with – you guessed it – Chinese restaurants, but it also has a smattering of Malaysian, Vietnamese, and Japanese eateries too.

The North End's vibe is almost exclusively Italian, from simple red-and-white-tablecloth cafés to sleek temples to regional *cucine*. For the trendiest dining spots, the South End and its SoWa (South of Washington) district are the places to head – between Tremont Street and Washington Avenue you will never go hungry.

Seafood, naturally, is a big feature of the Waterfront and up-and-coming Fort Point Channel areas, while the academic areas around Harvard and MIT are prime hunting grounds for good-value, atmospherically vibrant and cosmopolitan restaurants and cafés. Cambridge's reputation for healthy organic cooking is deserved, but the town is also no slouch at fine dining. When it comes to discovering hot new chefs, it is this side of the Charles River that often proves the more fertile.

ABUNDANT SEAFOOD

New England's seafood tradition is not to be confused with that of other American coastal regions, such as Louisiana or the Pacific Northwest. Fried clams, for instance, are nowhere better than along the North Shore of Massachusetts.

A drive along the Maine coast can become a movable feast of lobster; you can have it boiled and served roadside 'in the rough,' cubed or shredded with lashings of mayonnaise or melted butter in bulging rolls, or in rich bisques and stews. Wellfleet oysters, Chatham scallops from Cape Cod, freshly caught swordfish and bluefish are all considered to be among the world's greatest saltwater treats.

You should not miss out on trying authentic chowder packed with clams. You will also come across 'steamers,' soft-shelled clams so called because they are steam-cooked. Hard-shell clams come in several varieties, such as littlenecks, cherrystones, and quahogs.

Thanksgiving
The first Thanksgiving was celebrated in Plymouth in 1621 by the 50 or so *Mayflower* Pilgrims who had survived the initial year in New England. It has since become a tradition, complete with turkey, cranberries, and corn – all staple New England ingredients.

Left: Boston's North End is the place to go for Italian cooking.

Select Scrod

The term 'scrod' is used for white-fleshed fish. One story has it that the word sprung from the acronym for Select Catch Remains On Deck, the appellation sea captains would give to the best batches of fish.

Below: Boston's top ale.

CULINARY SPECIALTIES

When it comes to culinary curiosities, New England certainly has its share. All of the following can be found in the region: French Canadian-style breakfasts, with baked beans crowding eggs and sausages; clam pizza in Connecticut; vinegar-marinated Portuguese pork and seafood dishes that are especially common in southeastern Massachusetts; and muffins (or pancakes) packed with blueberries, which can frequently be purchased from roadside outlets in Maine.

Dairy Specialties

The milk from the many cows you will spot grazing pastures in Vermont is used to produce some of the region's best cheese. Cabot (www. cabotcheese.coop) is the big producer of Vermont cheddar; you will find a wide selection of their products at Quechee Gorge Village near Woodstock. You should also sample the quality dairy products of Shelburne Farms (see p. 78). The milk is not just used for cheese; Ben Cohen and Jerry Greenfield started making their now-famous crazy-flavoured ice creams in Vermont in 1978; drop by their factory in Waterbury (www.benjerry. com) for a tour.

WHERE TO EAT

New England has its fair share of fancy restaurants, ranging from the paneled elegance of old-school places such as Boston's Locke-Ober (see p.115) or Providence's Local 121 (see p.65) to the more relaxed, cutting-edge operations of Portland, Maine, or Portsmouth, New Hampshire.

If you are after a quick, cheap bite, you can hardly do better – or have a more authentic American dining experience – than at a diner. The diner phenomenon was born in Providence, Rhode Island, and matured in Worcester, Massachusetts, where the Worcester Lunch Car Company churned out over 600 pre-fabricated units up until the early

1960s. They are great places for breakfast; for one incorporating choice local products, head to The Farmers Diner *(see p.75)*. T. J. Buckley's in Brattleboro *(see p.118)* brings it full circle by using a handsomely renovated 1927 diner as a base for its fine-dining experience.

WHAT TO DRINK

When it comes to soft drinks, perhaps the one most associated with New England is cranberry juice; drive along Cape Cod to view the many cranberry bogs from which the luscious crimson berries are harvested each fall. There is even a cranberry festival held each year in Carver, Massachusetts (www.edaville.com). Spiked with vodka, the juice becomes a cocktail known as a Cape Coder.

Cafés and Coffee Milk

Café culture is alive and healthy throughout New England – in the college towns in particular you will seldom have to search far for a quirky, characterful joint in which to sip your morning brew, rather than an identikit Starbucks. While in Rhode Island, though, those with a sweet tooth might want to sample coffee milk, a mix of milk and syrupy condensed black coffee. The drink caught on after Italian immigrants introduced it to locals in the 1920s. It has become so popular that it was declared the state's official drink in 1993.

Beers and Microbrews

Founding father Samuel Adams was a brew master, so it is natural that one of Boston's principal breweries should have adopted his name. It started as a microbrewery in 1985; you will now find the fine range of Sam Adams ales (www.samueladams.com) in bars across the region. The other Boston beermaker that has hit the big time is Harpoon (www.harpoonbrewery.com); drop by their brewery for tours and tastings.

Boston microbreweries that have stayed micro include Boston Beer Works (www.beerworks.net), with branches near Fenway Park and the North End, and Cambridge Brewing Company (www.cambrew.com) near MIT. Vermont also has a thriving microbrewery industry; join Burlington Brew Tours (tel: 802-760-6091; www.burlingtonbrewtours.com) for a tour around four of the Lake Champlain area breweries.

Wine

You may be surprised to discover that New England has a small wine industry. From Newport in Rhode Island, you can follow the Coastal Wine Trail of Southeastern New England (www.coastalwinetrail.com), taking in eight wineries. Connecticut also promotes a wine trail (www.ctwine.com), covering 19 of the state's vineyards, and while you are up in Maine you might want to sample the wines flavored with local blueberries and other fruits.

Above from far left: Modern Diner, a 1941 Sterling Streamliner, in Pawtucket, Rhode Island; the Top of the Hub (tel: 617-536-1775; www.topofthehub.net) restaurant in Boston's Prudential Tower is on the expensive side, but has a fantastic view for drinks and nibbles at sundown.

SHOPPING

From enormous malls packed with famous labels to dusty antiques shops and cozy craft-stores to specialty shops selling outdoor gear, New England offers a wealth of shopping opportunities.

Art in Portland
Portland, Maine, has developed a reputation of late for its art scene. You can browse many commercial galleries in and around the city's Old Port District, where you will also find fine local pottery at the Maine Potters Market (www.maine pottersmarket.com).

Brimfield Antiques
Several times each year, the western Massachusetts town of Brimfield hosts New England's biggest antiques event (www.brimfieldshow. com). Hundreds of dealers converge to trade with each other and sell their wares to the public.

Opposite: antiques store in Wiscasset, Midcoast Maine.

BOSTON SHOPS

For the most comprehensive range of shopping, the region's biggest city, Boston, can't be beaten. Back Bay, with its Newbury Street couturiers and upscale Prudential Center and Copley Place shops (such as Lord & Taylor, Sacks Fifth Avenue, and Nieman-Marcus) is the main area to head, while Downtown there's Faneuil Hall Marketplace, featuring dozens of specialty shops in restored historic buildings.

ANTIQUES

Having been settled for nearly 400 years, New England was the first part of the country to realize that a fortune was hidden in its attics and basements. In Boston, antique dealers are clustered along Charles Street in Beacon Hill. Specialties of the district include high-end furniture, porcelain and silver, and marine paintings (although most of the city's most respected antique-art dealers are on Newbury Street in Back Bay).

Outside the city, eastern Massachusetts's biggest concentration of dealers is in the North Shore town of Essex, where at least a score of shops specialize in fine English furniture and 18th-century New England pieces, as well as the bizarre and funky. Out on Cape Cod, in Provincetown, dealers tend to favor camp and kitsch items from the mid-20th century.

Newfane, Vermont, has a fine concentration of antique shops, while down in Connecticut the towns of Putnam, New Preston, Woodbury, and Old Saybrook have all attracted a phalanx of dealers.

ARTS AND CRAFTS

New England's tradition of fine craftsmanship dates back to colonial times, when things were handmade by necessity. For beautiful examples of this type of work, head to the Hancock Shaker Village *(see p.62)*, where excellent modern reproductions of the religious sect's cherrywood boxes, handmade brooms, functional furniture, and other crafts are on sale.

The region continues to attract and inspire artisans who want to live and work in a place where they can absorb inspiration from the past, and find a ready market among quality-conscious locals and visitors. The League of New

Hampshire Craftsmen is an association of Granite State artisans – potters, jewelers, woodworkers, glass blowers, and weavers – who sell their work at six state locations, including the league's place of origin, Center Sandwich *(see p.81)*. Similarly, the Vermont State Craft Center Frog Hollow *(see p.76)* in Burlington, selects the best work by Vermont artisans.

Fine glassware is associated with Sandwich on Cape Cod. You can watch glass being hand-blown by Pairpoint Glass (www.pairpoint.com) in nearby Sagamore, which lays claim to being America's oldest glassworks. Handcrafted glass- and tableware form the centerpiece of the elegant complex of water-powered workrooms, shop, and restaurant at Simon Pearce (www.simonpearce.com) in Quechee, Vermont.

SPECIALTY SHOPPING

Some New England specialty stores have become destinations in themselves. Orvis (www.orvis.com) in Manchester, New Hampshire, has a country-chic persona built around its handmade fly rods and fishing tackle. In Maine, Kittery Trading Post (www.kitterytradingpost.com) will outfit a country expedition with nearly as much panache as at L.L. Bean *(see p.89)*.

Yankee Candle (www.yankeecandle.com) in Deerfield, Massachusetts, is a vast emporium of candles and gifts. Peter Limmer & Sons (www.limmercustomboot.com) in Intervale, New Hampshire, make fine hiking boots. And if you can't find a special item anywhere else, be sure to try Vermont Country Store in Weston *(see p.74)*.

Above from far left: traditional candle-making at Yankee Candle; Faneuil Hall Marketplace; in Boston you can kit yourself out in Red Sox baseball gear at the team store (19 Yawkey Way).

Opening Hours
Most stores open Monday to Saturday 9am to 7pm, and shopping malls generally stay open until 9pm. On Sunday opening hours are typically noon to 5pm or 6pm. Many smaller, independently owned shops are closed on Sunday.

Outlet Shopping

New England's factory-outlet phenomenon has two points of origin. One was the availability of inexpensive floor space in once-thriving mill towns, such as Fall River, Massachusetts. The other factor was the success of outdoor equipment and clothing supplier L.L. Bean; its 24-hour-a-day store in Freeport, Maine, drew so many visitors that other retailers moved in for a share of the market. Today, scores of top-name purveyors of men's and women's clothing, housewares, and gifts have set up shop in downtown Freeport, where you can find bargains on overstock, last-season, and second-quality items. The formula has been adopted in North Conway, New Hampshire; Manchester, Vermont; Kittery, Maine; Wrentham and Lee, Massachusetts; and Clinton, Connecticut.

SPORTS AND OUTDOOR ACTIVITIES

New Englanders are passionate about sport, with baseball being the game most enthusiastically supported. The region's great outdoors also provides a stage for a range of adventurous activities, from whale-watching to snowboarding.

SPECTATOR SPORTS

Generally, when it comes to watching top-league spectator sport in New England you are going to be heading to Boston. Among the city's various teams, it is the baseball-playing Red Sox who are the superstars, more for their fateful history than consistent wins.

Baseball

In 2004 the city's Major League baseball team finally broke the losing 'curse' in the World Series championships that had haunted them for 86 years – ever since the legendary slugger Babe Ruth was sold to eternal rivals, the New York Yankees. To prove their new-found form, the Red Sox (www.redsox.com) snatched another World Series victory in 2007, much to the delight of Bostonians who turned out en masse to welcome their heroes home in a tickertape parade.

Football

The Red Sox can now proudly stand shoulder to shoulder with the city's American football team, the New England Patriots (www.patriots.com). Three-time winners of the Super Bowl, the Patriots came close to winning a fourth time in 2008. Their home ground is the Gillette Stadium at Foxborough, 32 miles (51.5km) south of Boston, and the season runs from late August to late December. (Also playing at the Gillette Stadium is the professional soccer team New England Revolution; www.revolutionsoccer.net.)

Ice Hockey and Basketball

From October to mid-April in the T.D. Banknorth Garden stadium above Boston's North Station, you can catch games either by the city's ice-hockey team, the Bruins (www.bostonbruins.com), or the basketball team, the Celtics (www.nba.com/celtics).

For all the hoopla over the Red Sox, it is the Celtics who are the most successful team in any major sport in the country. Beginning in 1959, they won an unprecedented eight National Basketball Association (NBA) championships on the trot, and to date have 17 NBA wins to their credit, the most recent in 2008.

Boston Marathon
With over 30,000 runners, including Olympic champions, the Boston Marathon (www.bostonmarathon.com) is the world's oldest annually contested long-distance running race, the first one taking place back in 1867.

OUTDOOR ACTIVITIES

New England is a dream destination for those who desire an activity-driven vacation. Miles of coastlines and islands, not to mention multiple rivers and lakes, mean that sailing, canoeing, kayaking, and white-water rafting are all possibilities. The oceans also provide a venue for one of the most thrilling of wildlife displays – sightings of whales *(see feature)*. Fly- and deep-sea fishing are also popular pursuits.

The mountains and forest of Maine, Massachusetts, New Hampshire, and Vermont are the perfect settings for winter skiing vacations; head to mega resorts, such as Bretton Woods *(see p.84)*, Killington *(see p.74)*, and Loon *(see p.82)*, as well as Stowe, home of the Trapp Family Lodge (www.trapp family.com) of *The Sound of Music* fame. Come summer, the same locations are ideal for hiking and mountain biking.

Hiking and Climbing

In New Hampshire's Franconia Notch State Park *(see p.82)*, you can tackle an 8-mile (13km) section of the 2,175-mile (3,500km) long Appalachian Trail (www.nps.gov/appa), which runs across all the New England states bar Rhode Island. To find out more about this, the first National Scenic Trail, contact the Appalachian Trail Conservancy (www.appalachiantrail.org).

North Conway *(see p.85)* is a center for outdoor pursuits in New Hampshire; here you will find the International Mountain Climbing School (www.ime-usa.com), as well as the Eastern Mountain Sports Climbing School (www.ems climb.com), with several other locations around New England.

Not to be missed is spectacular Acadia National Park *(see p.93)*, the only such park in New England, threaded through with 115 miles (185km) of hiking trails. Equally impressive are the dunes and beaches of the Cape Cod National Seashore, covering the entire eastern shoreline of the Outer Cape *(see p.59)*.

Whale-Watching

The humpback gathering at the fertile feeding-ground Stellwagen Bank, 25 miles (40km) off the Boston coast, is one of the greatest in the world. Minkie whales can be seen too. Boston Harbor Cruises (tel: 617-227-4320; www.bostonharborcruises.com) and New England Aquarium Whale Watch (tel: 617-973-5277; www.neaq.org/visit/wwatch) run whale-watching tours from Boston's Long and Central wharves respectively.

The season runs from April to October, with the peak around June. Cruises take around three hours, and commentary is provided by naturalists. The water can be rough, so it is worth carrying anti-seasickness tablets. Rainwear is useful in April and May, and you should dress warmly even in summer. Whale-watching tours also depart from Gloucester, Plymouth, and Provincetown.

ENTERTAINMENT

Serious music, dance, and theater performances take place throughout New England. There is also a lively popular-music scene with many small clubs and venues, and a packed summer schedule of arts festivals.

Listings

For Nightlife listings, see pp.120–3.

In Boston, pick up a free copy of either *The Phoenix* (www. bostonphoenix.com) or *Weekly Dig* (www. weeklydig.com) to see who and what is playing around Boston, as well as for the lowdown on the hottest clubs.

Boston Tickets

The Bostix booths beside Faneuil Hall (Tue–Sat 10am–6pm, Sun 11am–4pm; ww.bostix.org) and on the corner of Copley Square (Mon–Sat 10am–6pm, Sun 11am–4pm) sell half-price tickets for many events (cash only) on performance day.

BOSTON

Given Boston's reputation as a bastion of high culture, and the presence of so many institutions of higher learning, including the respected Berklee College of Music *(see p.120)*, it is no wonder that the city is blessed with a vibrant performing-arts scene and a diverse range of entertainment venues.

Classical Music, Opera, and Dance

For classical music, review the concert schedule for the beautiful Symphony Hall *(see p.120)*, which hosts the world-class Boston Symphony Orchestra (BSO; www.bso.org), founded in 1881, from November to May. The orchestra can occasionally be heard playing outdoors at the Hatch Shell in the Esplanade beside the Charles River, where you may also catch the BSO's spin-off Boston Pops Orchestra. Every summer the BSO decamps to the Berkshires, where it headlines the Tanglewood Music Festival *(see feature, opposite)*.

Another excellent venue is Jordan Hall at the New England Conservatory of Music *(see p.121)*, which stages many free concerts, alongside ones by established ensembles such as the Boston Philharmonic (tel: 617-236-0999; www.bostonphil.org).

Opera, not Boston's strong point, is covered by the Boston Lyric Opera (tel: 617-542-4912; www.blo.org) and the Boston Opera (tel: 617-451-3388; www.operaboston.org). However, the Boston Ballet (tel: 617-695-6955; http://bostonballet.org) is one of the top dance companies in the US.

Rock and Pop

The stars of rock and pop regularly turn up at the city's biggest venues, such as the outdoor Bank of America Pavilion (www.livenation.com; May–September only) out on South Boston Waterfront, and T.D. Banknorth Garden (www.tdbanknorth garden.com), or medium-sized spaces such as the shabby-chic Orpheum Theater (tel: 617-679-0810; www.orpheum-theater.com).

However, with all those students around, there is an enormous range of small live-music venues and a thriving indie-rock scene of bands and singers to fill them. Check out places such as T.T. the Bear's Place and Paradise Rock Club *(see p.121)*.

Theater

Boston has a small but lively theater scene, with the city's grandest theaters such as the Wang and the Shubert (both part of the Citi Performing Arts Center; *see p.120*) often used for try-outs of Broadway-bound productions. The city's equivalent of *The Mousetrap* is the comic whodunit *Shear Madness*, staged since 1980 at the Charles Playhouse, where you can also catch the long-running Blue Man Group. For theater and ticket information, see www.boston-theater.com.

The most reliable places for interesting productions are The American Repertory Theatre (tel: 617-547-8300; www.amrep.org) over in Harvard, the Huntington (tel: 617-266-0800; www.huntingtontheatre.org) and the Boston Center for the Arts (tel: 617-426-5000; www.bcaonline.org), with four stages.

OUTSIDE BOSTON

New Haven, home to Yale University, also has a prestigious arts scene, with its New Haven Symphony Orchestra (tel: 203-776-1444; www.newhavensymphony.org) and several theaters, including Yale Repertory Theatre *(see p.123)*, where you can catch budding stars from the Yale School of Drama.

Elsewhere, the region's top cultural offerings tend to cluster in college towns and large cities. Connecticut's Hartford Symphony (tel: 860-244-2999; www.hartfordsymphony.org),

Maine's Portland Symphony Orchestra (tel: 207-773-6128; www.portlandsymphony.com), the Vermont Symphony Orchestra (tel: 802-864-5741; www.vso.org), and the Rhode Island Philharmonic (tel: 401-248-7000; www.ri-philharmonic.org) perform at home and throughout their respective states.

Summer Arts Festivals

There are several major arts festivals held each summer in the Berkshires, which are well worth planning your trip around. The Jacob's Pillow Dance Festival (tel: 413-243-0745; www.jacobspillow.org) held in Becket, 10 miles (16km) east of Lee, runs from June to August. Ballet, modern, and folk troupes perform on indoor and outdoor stages.

A mile out of central Lenox *(see p.62)* is the 400-acre (160ha) Tanglewood Estate (297 West Street; tel: 413-637-1600). Since 1934 this has been the summer home of the Boston Symphony Orchestra. From late June to early September, the prestigious Tanglewood Music Festival (www.bso.org) is held here, ranging from classical to jazz and blues. Pack a picnic and arrive a few hours before a performance to enjoy the magical atmosphere. Also in summer, Lenox hosts the Shakespeare & Co. Drama Festival (tel: 413-637-3353; www.shakespeare.org), including some free events.

HISTORY: KEY DATES

The region has been shaped by the blending and clashing of old England traditions and New World values, from the arrival of the Pilgrims in 1620, through the Salem witch trials and the Revolution, to today's mass tourism.

PRE-REVOLUTIONARY NEW ENGLAND

1602	The English explorer Captain Bartholomew Gosnold sights Cape Cod and Martha's Vineyard.
1614	Captain John Smith voyages down the coasts of Maine and Massachusetts and dubs the area New England.
1620	The *Mayflower* Pilgrims arrive at Plymouth.
1623	The first English settlements are established in New Hampshire.
1630	Puritan settlers establish the Boston and Massachusetts Bay Company.
1633–6	The first English settlements are set up in Connecticut (chartered 1662).
1636	Harvard College, the nation's first institution of higher learning, is founded at Cambridge, Massachusetts. Religious dissident Roger Williams founds the Rhode Island colony (chartered 1663).
1675–7	King Philip's War pits Wampanoag and Narragansett Indians against the colonists.
1692	Twenty people are executed for witchcraft at Salem, Massachusetts.
1704	French and allied Indians stage the Deerfield Raid, killing many settlers and taking captives to Canada.
1724	The first permanent European settlement is established in Vermont.
1754–63	The French and Indian War, with New England fighting on the British side, ends France's American empire.
1765	The Stamp Act tax stirs anti-British feeling.

THE BATTLE FOR INDEPENDENCE

1770	British soldiers fire upon the mob, killing five, in the 'Boston Massacre.'
1775	The American Revolution begins with the battles of Lexington and Concord. The Battle of Bunker Hill follows in June.
1776	The British are driven from Boston.
1783	The American Revolution ends.
1791	Vermont becomes the 14th state.

19TH CENTURY

1812–14 War with Britain.

1820 Maine, which was part of Massachusetts, becomes a separate state.

1822 The Merrimack Manufacturing Company is founded at Lowell, Massachusetts; it becomes harbinger of the region's industrial prowess.

1830–6 The first New England railroads link Boston with outlying cities.

1845–50 Boston is the destination of thousands fleeing Ireland's potato famine; the newcomers herald a radical change in the city's ethnic composition.

1861–5 Staunchly abolitionist New England sends troops to fight in the Civil War; Vermont suffers the highest casualty rate in the Union.

20TH CENTURY

*c.*1900 Amoskeag Mills in Manchester, New Hampshire, constitute the largest textile producer in the world.

1934 The advent of the first mechanical ski tow in Vermont; huge regional industry develops after World War II.

1935 Amoskeag Mills close, as the textile industry moves south.

1960 Bostonian John F. Kennedy is elected president; he establishes Cape Cod National Seashore to preserve undeveloped Cape lands.

1960s High-tech industry booms along Massachusetts's Route 128, thereby transforming the region's economic complexion.

1990s Severe limitations are imposed on cod fishing in response to dwindling stocks; numerous traditional livelihoods are threatened.

1999 Vermont adopts 'civil unions' as a legal form of gay partnerships; five years later Massachusetts becomes the first state to legalize gay marriage.

21ST CENTURY

2004 The Boston Red Sox break an 87-year losing streak by winning the World Series. Harvard students set up the social-networking site Facebook.

2006 Deval Patrick is elected Massachusetts governor, becoming only the second black governor in the US.

2008 Barack Obama wins all six states in the November election.

2009 New Hampshire becomes the sixth US state to allow same-sex couples to wed, bringing it into line with Connecticut, Maine, Massachusetts, and Vermont.

Above from far left: settlers mingle with natives at Plimoth Plantation; Battle of Lexington in 1775.

WALKS AND TOURS

BOSTON

The Freedom Trail, running from Boston Common to Charlestown, is lined with notable sites that recall the city's Revolutionary history. En route, the North End, Boston's Little Italy, is a great place to eat and drink.

State House
At the crest of Beacon Street, on the north-west edge of Boston Common, is the Massachusetts State House (tel: 617-727-3676; www.sec. state.ma.us; guided tours Mon–Fri 10am–4pm; free), designed by pre-eminent city architect Charles Bulfinch and completed in 1798. Dubbed 'the Hub of the Solar System' by Oliver Wendell Holmes (which later morphed into the city's nickname), this regal building's most visually impressive feature, the glittering dome crowned in gold leaf in 1861, was originally covered with shingles.

DISTANCE 5½ miles (8.75km)
TIME A full day
START Boylston T Station
END Community College T Station
POINTS TO NOTE

Downtown is busy with office workers Monday to Friday, particularly around lunchtime, so a good time to start this walk is early morning after rush hour or at the weekend. On Friday and Saturday there is also a lively fresh produce market near Haymarket T Station. The North End, Boston's Little Italy, is a good area to return to in the evening for dinner.

Boston's main Visitor Information Booth (tel: 617-536-4100; www. bostonusa.com; daily 8.30am–5pm) is located on the northeast edge of Boston Common just south of the Park Street T Station. You can pick up free maps here or book a place on one of the daily tours offered by the Freedom Trail Foundation (tel: 617-357-8300; www.thefreedomtrail.org), which begin from here.

Capital of Massachusetts, Boston likes to think of itself as the 'Cradle of Liberty' or the 'Hub of the Universe,' a city where modern America started and found its distinctive, independent voice. This walk, which shadows the Freedom Trail, features significant landmarks that figured in the decisive break that New England's settlers made from the British in 1776. Established in 1958 to preserve these key monuments and sites, the trail is marked by a red-brick or painted line on the pavement.

BOSTON COMMON AND DOWNTOWN

From Boylston T Station, walk to **Boston Common ❶**, established in 1634 and the oldest public park in the US. Originally used as a 'Comon Field' *(sic)* on which sheep and cattle grazed (they did so up until 1830), the pentagonal space, covering about 50 acres (20ha), was also used as a mustering ground for militias and a venue for public hangings. Within the common, you will find the **Central Burying Ground ❷** (daily dawn–dusk), the city's fourth-oldest cemetery; the 70ft

(21m) **Soldiers and Sailors Monument ③**, dedicated to the Union forces killed in the Civil War; and **Frog Pond ④**, used as a children's wading pool in summer and an ice rink in winter.

Park Street

On the corner of Park and Tremont streets stands **Park Street Church ⑤** (tel: 617-523-3383; www.parkstreet.org; mid-June–Aug Tue–Sat 9.30am–3.30pm; free), with its majestic 217ft (66m) steeple adapted from a Christopher Wren design. William Lloyd Garrison delivered his first anti-slavery speech here in 1829.

Next to the church on Tremont Street, pay your respects at the graves of Paul Revere, Samuel Adams, John Hancock, and other key revolutionary figures in the illustrious **Old Granary Burying Ground ⑥** (9am–5pm, winter until 3pm), dating from 1660.

King's Chapel and Burying Ground

On the corner of School and Tremont streets is **King's Chapel ⑦** (tel: 617-523-1749; www.kings-chapel.org; July–Aug daily 10am–4pm, other months Sat 10am–4pm, Sun 1.30–4pm; services Wed 12.15pm and Sun 11am; free). The present granite structure dates from 1754, but the chapel had its origins in the 1680s, when Britain's King James II made a colossal political blunder by sending to Boston a clergyman whose job was to install in the

town the very thing the Puritans had hated and fled: a branch of the Church of England.

Next to the chapel, on Tremont Street, is Boston's first cemetery, **King's Chapel Burying Ground** (daily 9am–5pm, winter until 3pm), in

Above from far left: just across Charles Street from the common is the glorious Public Garden; ornate ceiling in the Massachusetts State House.

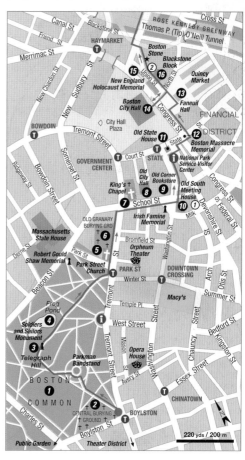

Above from left:
King's Chapel Burying Ground; Old City Hall.

use from 1630 to 1796. The Bay Colony's first governor, John Winthrop, was buried here in 1649.

Old City Hall

Farther along School Street is **Old City Hall** ❽ (tel: 617-523-8678; www.oldcityhall.com), built in 1865 in the French Second Empire style. When the city government decamped from here in 1969 for the new City Hall *(see right)*, this handsome edifice was preserved as a mixed-use complex of offices and a restaurant. In the forecourt are bronze statues of Benjamin Franklin and Josiah Quincy, in his time a senator, Boston mayor and president of Harvard.

Old Corner Bookstore

At the intersection of School and Washington streets is the **Old Corner Bookstore** ❾, dating from 1712, and currently a jeweler's. Over the years the building has served as an apothecary, a dry goods store, and a private residence, although it's fondly remembered in its 1828 incarnation as the home of the eminent Ticknor and Fields publishing firm and a bookstore. In the Golden Age of American literature, the store was a popular meeting place for John Greenleaf Whittier, Ralph Waldo Emerson, Harriet Beecher Stowe, Louisa May Alcott and other distinguished writers.

Old South Meeting House

Immediately to the right on Washington Street is the **Old South Meeting House** ❿ (tel: 617-482-6439; www.oldsouthmeetinghouse. org; daily Apr–Oct 9.30am–5pm, Nov–Mar 10am–4pm; charge), built in 1727 and styled after the graceful London chapels of Sir Christopher Wren. The church was the scene of the events that preceded the infamous Boston Tea Party of 1773 and the baptism on a chilly January 6, 1706, of Benjamin Franklin, born around the corner on Milk Street, where you will find the **Milk Street Café**, see ⑪①.

Boston Tea Party
It was at the Old South Meeting House *(pictured right)* that, on December 16, 1773, more than 5,000 Bostonians met to decide what to do with three tea-laden ships in the harbor. Disguised as Mohawk Indians, a gang of colonists, enraged at the British tax placed on tea and other imports, ran down Milk Street to Griffins Wharf. The crowd followed and, with cries of 'Boston harbor a teapot tonight!', 340 crates of tea were dumped overboard.

Old State House

From the Old South Meeting House continue north along Washington Street toward the junction with State Street. Immediately to the right, overshadowed by modern skyscrapers, is the **Old State House** ⓫ (tel: 617-720-3290; www.bostonhistory.org; daily 9am–5pm, June–late Aug until 6pm; charge), Boston's oldest public building, built in 1713 as the seat of the colonial government, and now a small museum displaying items relating to Boston's role in the Revolutionary War and other parts of the city's history.

Boston Massacre

It is easy to miss the circle of cobblestones on a tiny traffic island at the junction of State and Congress streets. This marks the spot of the **Boston Massacre** ⓬, where on March 5, 1770, a handful of British soldiers fired into a jeering crowd that was pelting them with snowballs; five men were killed, including one former slave, Crispus Attucks, who is buried in the Old Granary Burying Ground *(see p.29)*.

Faneuil Hall and Quincy Market

Head north on Congress Street and turn right to reach **Faneuil Hall** ⓭ (tel: 617-242-5642; www.faneuilhall.com; daily 9.30am–4.30pm; free). A statue of Samuel Adams, one of the founding fathers of the United States, stands in front of the former public hall, which was named for benefactor Peter Faneuil.

Designated by patriot orator James Otis as the 'Cradle of Liberty,' it was here that the Sons of Liberty called many meetings complaining about British taxation without representation. On the building's lower floors are many touristy shops, more of which you will find in the adjacent **Quincy Market** complex. The latter is named for mayor Josiah Quincy, who came up with the idea for the 1826-vintage marketplace. Much like London's Covent Garden, meat and produce were sold here for 150 years before the buildings were renovated to host the scores of souvenir stalls and boutiques found today.

Boston City Hall

On the west side of Congress Street climb the concrete steps leading up to **Boston City Hall** ⓮. Prior to the construction in 1969 of this charmless inverted ziggurat, the area was known as Scollay Square, a slightly disreputable entertainment area. In the

The Historic T

Opened in 1897, 'Park Street Under' was the first subway station in the US. The subway is now run by Massachusetts Bay Transport Authority (MBTA); *see p.105*. Most Bostonians simply call it 'The T', after the system's logo: a T in a circle.

Food and Drink 🍴

① MILK STREET CAFE
50 Milk Street; tel: 617-542-3663; www.milkstreetcafe.com; Mon–Fri 7am–3pm; $
Reasonable prices for generous portions is the deal at this kosher cafeteria with dairy and fish, but no meats. You can sample made-from-scratch dishes, such as roasted salmon salad and vegetable lasagne, and nutritious homemade soups.

Visitor Center

Opposite the Old State House is the National Park Service Visitor Center (15 State Street; tel: 617-242-5642; www.nps.gov/bost; daily 9am–5pm), a valuable source of information and literature. Rangers lead free daily walking tours along part of the Freedom Trail from here.

Above from left:
celebrating a *festa* in the North End; view of the North End from St Stephen's Church to the Old North Church; New England Holocaust Memorial.

1960s the Boston Redevelopment Authority decided to raze Scollay Square and the nearby tenements of the West End. The area was renamed Government Center, its focus the vast, bleak City Hall Plaza.

New England Holocaust Memorial

Beautiful in a melancholy way are the six tall, slender glass-and-steel towers of the **New England Holocaust Memorial** 🅑 in Carmen Park, a strip of greenery opposite the City Hall between Union and Congress streets. Forming a mute tribute to the those murdered by the Nazis in World War II, each glass column, wreathed in steam symbolizing the gas chambers, represents a different concentration camp and is inscribed with numbers – 6 million in total.

Blackstone Block

In stark contrast to the concrete waste-lands of Government Center are the charming brick buildings and cobbled lanes, dating back to the 17th century, of **Blackstone Block** 🅖, named for Boston's first colonist, William Blackstone (who settled in the Boston Common area in 1625). The block is bounded by Union, Hanover, Blackstone, and North streets. At 41 Union Street is the historic **Union Oyster House**, see ⑪②.

A few yards down Marshall Street, opposite the 18th-century Ebenezer Hancock House at no. 10, look down to see the **Boston Stone**, a stone ball and trough built into the wall of a gift shop. Shipped from England in 1700 to serve as a paint mill, the stones were later used as the point from which all distances from Boston were measured. Their role as the hub of 'The Hub' was later taken over by the dome of the Massachusetts State House *(see margin, p.28)*.

If it is a Friday or Saturday you may want to linger around here to enjoy the **fresh produce market** that wraps its way around North and Blackstone streets. Otherwise, continue across the Rose Kennedy Greenway into the North End.

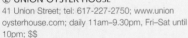

Food and Drink

② UNION OYSTER HOUSE
41 Union Street; tel: 617-227-2750; www.union oysterhouse.com; daily 11am–9.30pm, Fri–Sat until 10pm; $$
A favorite haunt of President Kennedy, this touristy restaurant has a top-class raw bar, and serves both seafood and steaks in atmospheric rooms with creaky floors, low ceilings, and wooden booths.

③ CAFFÉ PARADISO
255 Hanover Street, North End; tel: 617-742-1768; www.caffeparadiso.com; daily 6.30am–2am; $$
A popular local hangout, where the espressos, cannoli, panini, and calzones are all delicious. The television beams in soccer games from Italy via satellite.

④ CAFFÉ VITTORIA
290–296 Hanover Street, North End; tel: 617-227-7606; www.vittoriacaffe.com; daily 6am–midnight; $
This quintessential Italian café has quirky decor including almost a museum collection's worth of antique espresso machines. All kinds of beverages other than coffee are served along with traditional sweets.

THE NORTH END

Until only a few years ago the raised expanse of the Fitzgerald Expressway (also known as the Central Artery) cut the North End off from the rest of the city. Now that the 'Big Dig' has buried the road underground, the cleared land forms a ribbon of parks through the city known collectively as the **Rose Kennedy Greenway** ⑰, named for the mother of President John F. Kennedy, who was born in the North End in 1890. Railings either side of Hanover Street, as it cuts through the park, are inscribed with historical dates and quotations about the area from past residents.

Paul Revere House

The North End is Boston's Little Italy, and the central artery Hanover Street is almost wall-to-wall cafés and restaurants. For an espresso to power your way, pause at **Caffé Paradiso**, see ⑪③, or **Caffé Vittoria**, see ⑪④.

Turn right on Richmond Street and then left to enter cobbled North Square. Here, at no. 19, you will find the **Paul Revere House** ⑱ (tel: 617-523-2338; www.paulreverehouse.org; daily mid-Apr–Oct 9.30am–5.15pm, Nov–mid-Apr 9.30am–4.15pm; charge). Built in 1676, this two-story dwelling, with an overhanging second floor, is the oldest wooden house in downtown Boston. Revere, then a silversmith, took up residence in 1770, and it is

furnished today much as it was when it was home to him and the first Mrs Revere, who bore him eight children, and then, when she died, to the second Mrs Revere, who produced a similar brood. It is from here that Revere started his historic horse ride that warned, 'the British are coming!'

Pierce-Hichborn House

Next door is the restored **Pierce-Hichborn House** (guided tours only once or twice daily; call Paul Revere House for details), which belonged to Nathaniel Hichborn, Revere's cousin. The asymmetrical, three-story brick building, built between 1711 and 1715 in the new English Renaissance style, was a radical departure from the Tudor-style wooden dwellings built in the previous century.

St Stephen's Church

Exit North Square via Prince Street following the red bricks of the Freedom

Ye Olde House

Union Oyster House claims the title of Boston's oldest brick house. A rare example of Georgian architecture in the city, the restaurant dates to at least 1660, when it was owned by Boston's first town crier, William Courser. Mentioned in a city plan of 1708, the house was the office of the *Massachusetts Spy* newspaper from 1771 to 1775, while in 1776 the exiled Louis-Philippe, who later became king of France, taught French in the rooms above James Amblard's tailor shop.

Weekend Processions

If you are in Boston in summer, be sure to time your visit to the North End to catch one of the local Italian community's feasts or *festas*, celebrated in honor of saints' days. They are held almost every weekend in July and August, with Sunday being by far the more exciting day, and usually involve street fairs, brass bands, singers, raffles, food stalls selling sausage, peppers, and *zeppole* (fried dough), and processions in which saints' statues are carried, often festooned with contributions of paper money.

Trail back to Hanover Street. Turn right and walk two blocks north to reach white-steepled **St Stephen's Church ⑲**. Built in 1804 as a Congregationalist Meeting House, this dignified structure is the only one of five Boston churches designed by noted Boston architect Charles Bulfinch that still stands.

Paul Revere Mall

Directly opposite St Stephen's Church is the **Paul Revere Mall ⑳**, known locally as the Prado. Built in 1933, this spacious brick courtyard is one of the liveliest public spaces in the North End – a sort of Americanized piazza where kids run around, old folks play cards, and footsore tourists take a breather from the Freedom Trail. In addition to a traditional Italian fountain, the Prado features a magnificent equestrian statue of Paul Revere, modeled in 1885 by Cyrus Dallin and cast in 1940. On the south (left) wall, bronze panels recall the history of Boston and its people.

Old North Church

At the far end of the Prado a small gate opens to the rear of Christ Church, more popularly known as **Old North Church ㉑** (tel: 617-523-6676; www.oldnorth.com; June–Oct daily 9am–6pm, Nov–May Mon–Sat 9am–5pm, Sun 9–9.45am, 10.45am–12.15pm; free). Built in 1723, this is Boston's oldest church. Its interior, painted white since 1912, sports high pew boxes, designed to keep in the warmth of braziers filled with hot coal or bricks, which were placed on the floor in winter. The clock at the rear and the four Baroque Belgian cherubs that surround it date back to the opening of the church. So does the organ case, although the actual instrument dates only from 1759. It is still played at the service every Sunday at 11am.

Copp's Hill Burying Ground

On exiting from the church, walk up Hull Street for about 150yds/m to **Copp's Hill Burying Ground** ㉒ (daily dawn–dusk), Boston's second-oldest cemetery (after King's Chapel; *see p.29*), where the gravestones, some ornately carved, poke out of the grass like misshapen teeth. It is named for William Copp, who farmed on the hill's southeast slope in the mid-17th century. In the colonial period, the base of the hill, known pejoratively as New Guinea (after the African country of Guinea), was occupied by the city's first black community, and about 1,000 blacks are buried in the cemetery's northwest corner.

CHARLESTOWN

The Freedom Trail's red-brick route leads you down Hull Street to Commercial Street, where you turn left and then right to cross the Charles River on the **Charlestown Bridge** ㉓. Crossing the bridge (don't look down if you suffer from vertigo) provides an excellent view on the left-hand side of the **Charlestown Locks**, which control the water level between the river and the Inner Harbor, and, rising majestically in the background, the **Leonard P. Zakim Bunker Hill Bridge** (www.leonardp zakimbunkerhillbridge.org), one of the most striking contemporary structures in the city.

Paul Revere Park

Below the bridge on the Charlestown side of the river is pretty little **Paul Revere Park** ㉔. Take the steps down to the park and follow the walkway under the Charlestown Bridge and past the hotel on Tudor Wharf toward the Charlestown Navy Yard, before which you could take a breather at **Sorrelle**

Above from far left: St Stephen's Church; gravestone in Copp's Hill Burying Ground.

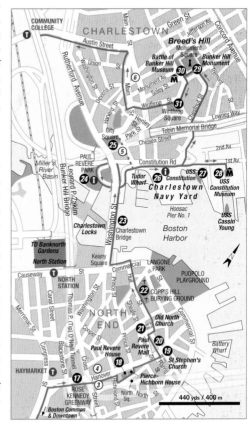

Above from left:
clapboard houses in the Bunker Hill neighborhood; all aboard the USS *Constitution*.

Bakery and Café, see 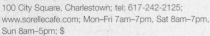, facing onto **City Square** ㉕. In the square's center a small circle of greenery preserves the foundations of the Great House, a structure dating from 1629 and believed to have been John Winthrop's home and the colony's brief seat of government.

Food and Drink 🍴

⑤ SORELLE BAKERY AND CAFÉ
100 City Square, Charlestown; tel: 617-242-2125; www.sorellecafe.com; Mon–Fri 7am–7pm, Sat 8am–7pm, Sun 8am–5pm; $
This more recently opened branch (the original is at 1 Monument Avenue) keeps longer hours and has trendier looks, but still serves incredible breads and pastries, fresh sandwiches and salads, and beverages.

⑥ WARREN TAVERN
2 Pleasant Street, Charlestown; tel: 617-241-8142; www.warrentavern.com; Mon–Fri 11.30am–1am, Sat–Sun 10.30am–1am; $
Named for Revolutionary hero General Warren, this historic pub has low ceilings and beams that make it a convivial spot for lunch. Burgers and chunky sandwiches are the specialty. There is live music some evenings.

Charlestown History

Established in 1628, two years ahead of Boston, Charlestown lays claim to being the city's oldest neighbourhood. In 1630 it was the seat of the British government, and on Breed's Hill the bloody Battle of Bunker Hill was fought on June 17, 1775. Its prosperity used to be tied up with the Navy Yard founded in 1800. At times (usually wartimes) it was the busiest shipbuilding and repair yards in the US, but in 1974 demand had slowed to the point where the facility was forced to close – a third of it was taken over by the National Park Service.

Charlestown Navy Yard

Back on Constitution Road, walk east toward the **Charlestown Navy Yard** ㉖, home to the USS *Constitution*. Just inside the entrance is the **Visitor Center** (tel: 617-242-5601; www.nps.gov/bost; daily Sept–June 9am–5pm, July–Aug 9am–6pm), where you can find out about free tours of the ship and its neighbor, the restored naval destroyer USS *Cassin Young*.

The **USS *Constitution*** ㉗ (www.ussconstitutionmuseum.org; Apr–Oct Tue–Sun, Nov–Mar Thur–Sun 10am–3.30pm; tours on the half-hour; donation welcome) is the world's oldest warship still in commission. It keeps this status thanks to an annual July 4 'turnaround,' when tugs pull 'Old Ironsides' out into the harbor.

Elsewhere in the Navy Yard is the **USS *Constitution* Museum** ㉘ (tel: 617-426-1812; www.ussconstitutionmuseum.org; daily mid-Apr–mid-Oct 9am–6pm, mid-Oct–mid-Apr 10am–5pm; donation welcome), which simulates the experience of life below decks.

Bunker Hill Monument and Museum

Exit the Navy Yard back onto Constitution Road and turn right to reach Chelsea Street. Duck through the nearby underpass beneath the Tobin Bridge, emerging on Lowney Way. Turn left and then immediately right onto Chestnut Street. Continue along Chestnut Street to the **Bunker Hill**

Monument 🔵 (daily 9am–4.30pm; free), a 220ft (67m) high granite obelisk crowning Breed's Hill. The battle was fought just north of the monument. Climb the 294 stairs to the top for rewarding views of the city.

On the corner of Monument Square and Monument Avenue is the small **Battle of Bunker Hill Museum** 🔵 (tel: 617-242-5641; www.nps.gov.bost; daily 9am–5pm; free) where, on the second floor, hangs an excellent reproduction of the *Bunker Hill Cyclorama*, a circular painting that places the viewer at the heart of the battle's action.

Winthrop Square

From the southeast corner of Monument Square, head downhill along Winthrop Street into picturesque **Winthrop Square** 🔵. For a century this was a training field where Charlestown boys learned the art of war. At the northwest corner notice the gate flanked by bronze tablets commemorating those killed on June 17, 1775.

Return to Winthrop Street and keep going downhill, past the fire station and across Warren Street until you reach the junction with Main Street. Turn right here and continue to the corner of Pleasant Street, where the historic **Warren Tavern**, see 🍴⑥, dates from 1780. Both Paul Revere and George Washington once stayed here.

From here, a short walk west along Austin Street and across busy Rutherford Avenue will bring you to Community College T Station, behind Bunker Hill Community College. Alternatively, amble back through Charlestown, admiring its many old homes, toward the North End, a pleasant place for an evening meal.

Below: Bunker Hill Monument.

HARVARD

This walking tour takes you around the university's hallowed halls, into some of its excellent museums, ranging from visual arts to archaeology and natural history, and back across the river for fantastic views.

DISTANCE 4 miles (6.5km)
TIME A full day including museum visits
START/END Harvard Square T Station
POINTS TO NOTE
It is difficult to do full justice to all of Harvard's museums in one day. Decide whether you would prefer a brief once-over of everything, or a concentrated session at, say, the natural history museums. Note that the Fogg Art and Busch-Reisinger museums are closed until 2013 (see p.40).

Below: graduation day; Harvard flag.

Many visitors associate Harvard with Boston, but the world-famous university is actually in the separate city of Cambridge, which lies on the north bank of the Charles River.

HARVARD YARD

Orientate yourself in **Harvard Square ❶**, which is actually an amorphous area rather than a four-sided square. To the west lies the Coop, or Harvard Cooperative Society (a bookstore and department store founded in 1882). To the east, **Harvard Yard** has the university's most historic buildings, bordered on the south and west by Massachusetts Avenue. The Yard is the geographic heart of America's oldest and most prestigious university, founded in 1636. Six of Harvard's graduates have become US president, and it has churned out dozens of Nobel and Pulitzer prizewinners.

'The Statue of Three Lies'

Enter Harvard Yard by the Johnston Gate, flanked on the right by **Massachusetts Hall** (1718) and on the left by **Harvard Hall**. Immediately ahead is **University Hall**, a white granite building designed by Charles Bulfinch in 1814. The bronze statue of John Harvard in front of University Hall is nicknamed 'The Statue of Three Lies,' because it is not of John Harvard, but of an 1884 undergraduate sculpted by Daniel French Chester; the inscription refers to John Harvard as founder of Harvard College, when he was in fact only the first major benefactor; and, contrary to the inscription, the college was not founded in 1638, the year of Harvard's bequest, but in 1636.

NEW YARD

Walk around University Hall into the Tercentenary Quadrangle, or **New Yard** ❷, which, on the first Monday of each June, is the scene of Commencement, Harvard's major graduation ceremony.

New Yard is dominated on the south by the **Widener Memorial Library** (closed to general public), with its grand Corinthian colonnade atop a monumental flight of stairs. Inside lies the third-largest library in the country and part of the largest university library in the world – 13 million volumes including a Gutenberg Bible and a First Folio of Shakespeare.

The north side of New Yard is punctuated by the soaring, delicate white spire of **Memorial Church**, which honors the Harvard dead in both world wars.

Above from far left:
Widener Memorial Library; students on the library steps.

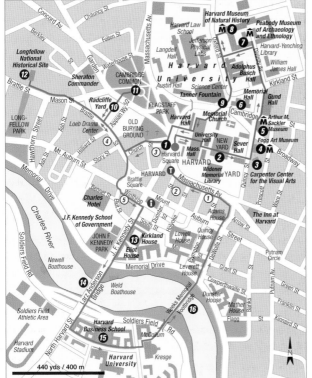

The Swimming Test
The Widener Library is named for Harvard graduate Harry Elkins Widener, who drowned along with his father when the *Titanic* sunk. Legend has it that when his mother donated $2 million to found the library, it was on condition that all Harvard undergraduates pass a 50-yard swimming test. However, the test, no longer administered, pre-dated Harry's attendance at Harvard.

New Art Museum

In 2008 the adjoining Fogg Art Museum and Busch-Reisinger Museum closed for major renovations. The plan is to bring the two art museums under the same roof as the Arthur M. Sackler Museum. The Harvard Art Museum, in a new building designed by Renzo Piano, is slated to open in 2013. During the construction period the Sackler's galleries have been reconfigured to show key pieces from the collections of the Fogg and the Busch-Reisinger.

On the east side of the Yard is the Romanesque **Sever Hall**, considered one of architect H.H. Richardson's finest works. Its entrance is flanked by turreted towers, and the entire building is wonderfully rich in decorative brickwork.

ART MUSEUMS

Walk behind Sever Hall to emerge on Quincy Street, where you will find yourself facing the strikingly modern **Carpenter Center for the Visual Arts** ❸ (tel: 617-495-3251; www.ves.fas. harvard.edu; usually Mon–Sat 1–5pm; free), the only Le Corbusier building in North America. The ground-floor and third-floor galleries host exhibitions by international artists.

Next door at no. 32 are the **Fogg Art Museum** and **Busch-Reisinger Museum** ❹, both currently closed for renovations until 2013 *(see margin, left)*. The highlights of the Fogg include works by Ingres, and a fine collection of Pre-Raphaelite and French Impressionist works. In addition, there are dozens of Blake watercolors, and hundreds of Dürer and Rembrandt prints. The Busch-Reisinger collection, specializing in art from the German-speaking countries of central and northern Europe, includes 20th-century Expressionist canvases by Klee and Kandinsky, as well as the archives of architects Gropius and Feininger, forming the largest Bauhaus collection outside Germany.

Arthur M. Sackler Museum

During the renovations, pieces from both collections are being displayed in rotation at the nearby **Arthur M. Sackler Museum** ❺ (485 Broadway; tel: 617-495-9400; www.harvardart museum.org; Mon–Sat 10am–5pm, Sun 1–5pm; charge), alongside an outstanding collection of Chinese jades. The Sackler's Ancient and Islamic collections are also noteworthy.

Lunch Options

Either before or after visiting the Sackler, you can backtrack down Quincy Street to Massachusetts Avenue for lunch. Turn right to find **Mr Bartley's Burger Cottage**, see ⑪①, or walk further down the avenue toward Harvard Square and turn left on Dunster Street to arrive at **B. Good**, see ⑪②.

Harvard Tours

For the inside scoop on Harvard, take one of the student-led tours of the campus (Feb–Apr and mid-Sept–mid-Dec Mon–Fri 10am and 2pm, Sat 2pm, mid-June–mid-Aug Mon–Sat 10 and 11.15am, 2 and 3.15pm; free), leaving from the Harvard University Information Center, Holyoke Center Arcade (1350 Massachusetts Avenue; tel: 617-495-1573; www.harvard.edu). A fun alternative is the 70-minute Unofficial Harvard Tour (tel: 617-848-8576; www.harv.un officialtours.com; Sat–Sun 10.45am, 12.45 and 1.45pm; donations welcome), which leaves from Harvard Square outside Harvard T Station.

MEMORIAL HALL

Return to Quincy Street and follow it north across Cambridge Street. On the left is **Memorial Hall ❻**, a huge, red-brick Victorian Gothic pile, dating from 1874, with polychromatic roofs, which contains the Sanders Theater, the university's largest auditorium. Its somewhat truncated appearance is the result of a fire that destroyed the tall pinnacled roof over the central tower. If the building is open, pop in to admire the stained-glass windows.

On the right of Memorial Hall is the contrasting slender-pillared **Gund Hall**, built in 1969, and home of the Graduate School of Design.

PEABODY MUSEUM

Cross Kirkland Street and enter Divinity Avenue. On the left side is the handsome, medieval-style **Adolphus Busch Hall** (named for the beer baron). Toward the end of the avenue, on the left at no. 11, is the fascinating **Peabody Museum of Archaeology and Ethnology ❼** (tel: 617-495-7535; www.peabody.harvard.edu; daily 9am–5pm; charge). Among its superb collection of artifacts from around the globe are the only surviving Native American objects gathered by the explorers Meriwether Lewis and William Clark, who led the first American overland expedition to the Pacific coast (1804–6), as well as a huge photographic archive.

MUSEUM OF NATURAL HISTORY

Leaving the Peabody, turn right and right again to follow the footpath around the building to Oxford Street. Here, turn right once more to reach the entrance of the **Harvard Museum of Natural History ❽** (tel: 617-495-3045; www.hmnh.harvard.edu; daily 9am–5pm; charge). Its most famous exhibit is the collection of over 3,000 extraordinarily lifelike handmade glass flowers. Kids will also love its collection of dinosaur remains, including a 12ft (3.5m) tall Plateosaurus.

TANNER FOUNTAIN

Exit back onto Oxford Street, and, turning left, continue past the Science Center, the largest building on Harvard campus. In front of it, amid a patch of

Above from far left: butterflies in the Museum of Natural History; Memorial Hall; the superb Peabody Museum.

Food and Drink

① MR BARTLEY'S BURGER COTTAGE
1246 Massachusetts Avenue; tel: 617-354-6559; www.bartleysburgers.com; Mon–Sat 11am–9pm; $
A Harvard institution, this classic mom-and-pop burger joint offers a wide range of burgers named for famous politicians like Bill Clinton and Arnold Schwarzenegger.

② B. GOOD
24 Dunster Street; tel: 617-354-6500; www.bgood.com; Mon–Sat 11am–10pm, Sun 11am–9pm; $
Few restaurants can truly claim they serve healthy junk food, but B. Good actually does. Lean meats are hand-packed to create a variety of delicious burger combos, and there are hand-cut baked fries and excellent salads. Eat in or take out.

grass to the north of Harvard Yard, stands the unusual **Tanner Fountain** ❾, gurgling amid a circular grouping of 159 boulders. Re-enter Harvard Yard and return to the Johnston Gate.

RADCLIFFE YARD

Cross Massachusetts Avenue and head west on Church Street. Just off to the left, on Palmer Street, is **Veggie Planet**, see Ⓨ③. Turn right at the junction with Brattle Street. Continue walking until you pass Appian Way. Next on the right is **Radcliffe Yard** ❿, which is sur-

rounded by a number of delightful late 19th- and early 20th-century buildings. This is where the renowned women's college of that name, now fully integrated with Harvard, began life in 1879.

Exit from the yard's far side onto Garden Street, which borders **Cambridge Common** ⓫. Surrounded by a semicircle of cannons, a bronze relief marks the spot where, on July 4, 1775, George Washington assumed command of the Continental Army.

LONGFELLOW HOUSE

Return through Radcliffe Yard to Brattle Street. Leafy and tranquil compared to the hubbub of Harvard Square, this prestigious street is lined by splendid clapboard houses fronted by elegant porticoes, most from the 19th century, some from even earlier.

The cream-colored clapboard building located at no. 105 is where Henry Wadsworth Longfellow (1807–82) composed many of his most famous works. It is now the **Longfellow National Historical Site** ⓬ (tel: 617-876-4491; www.nps.gov/long; June–Oct Wed–Sun noon–4.30pm; charge). Even if the house is closed, its pleasant grounds are always open for inspection.

Stroll back along Brattle Street toward Harvard Square, pausing either at **L.A. Burdick Chocolate Shop and Café**, see Ⓨ④, or **The Red House**, see Ⓨ⑤, across Brattle Square on Winthrop Street.

MIT

Harvard is not the only famous university in Cambridge. Hop on the T and emerge at Kendall/MIT station to explore the Massachusetts Institute of Technology (MIT). Founded in 1861, MIT's reputation for science research obscures the fact that there's a fair amount of support for the arts on campus too. The List Visual Arts Center (Wiesner Building, 20 Ames Street; tel: 617-253-4444; http://web.met.edu/lvac; Tue–Sun noon–6pm, Thur until 8pm; free) has temporary exhibits of outstanding contemporary art. In the west campus the Kresge Auditorium and the MIT Chapel are two outstanding buildings designed by a Finnish architect,

Eero Saarinen, while in the east campus is the whimsical Frank Gehry-designed Ray and Maria Stata Center. Go inside to pick up a self-guided tour leaflet of the campus from the information desk.

TOWARD THE CHARLES RIVER

From Winthrop Street turn right onto John F. Kennedy Street, and walk south past, on the left, the neo-Georgian **Kirkland House** ⓭ and **Eliot House**. Each residential co-ed house is a small college with about 400 students and its own administration, library, dining hall, exclusive societies and clubs, and a veritable phalanx of tutors.

On the other side of John F. Kennedy Street is Harvard's **John F. Kennedy School of Government** (www.hks.harvard.edu), fronted by the riverside John F. Kennedy Park.

Across busy Memorial Drive the handsome **Larz Anderson Bridge** ⓮, named in memory of Nicholas Longworth Anderson, a distinguished colonel in the US Civil War, spans the Charles River. From here, there are superb views of the college, and, in the foreground, the Weld Boathouse, home of Harvard's women's crew. The boathouse to the right is home to the men's crew.

HARVARD BUSINESS SCHOOL

Cross the river, and continue straight on what is now North Harvard Street for 100yds/m, passing on the right the Harvard playing fields and, on the left, the prestigious **Harvard Business**

School ⓯. Turn left and stroll through the campus. Here the neo-Georgian buildings display a consistent rhythm of green doors, white window-frames, and red-brick walls.

Emerging on the school's east side, take the footbridge over busy Soldiers Field Road to the **Weeks Memorial Footbridge** ⓰, which again offers an excellent view of some of Harvard's residential buildings.

Cross Memorial Drive and head north along DeWolfe Street aiming for Massachusetts Avenue, where a left turn will bring you back to Harvard Square.

Above from far left: on the banks of the Charles River; Longfellow House.

Food and Drink

③ VEGGIE PLANET

Club Passim, 47 Palmer Street; tel: 617-661-1513; www.veggieplanet.net; daily 11.30am–10.30pm; $

A vegetarian restaurant with social responsibility. Didi Emmons lives up to her reputation as one of the most inventive vegetarian chefs in the city by creating tasty meatless pizzas and vegan meals. In the evening there's folk music.

④ L.A. BURDICK CHOCOLATE SHOP AND CAFÉ

52-D Brattle Street; tel: 617-491-4340; www.burdick chocolate.com; Mon–Thur 8am–9pm, Fri–Sat 8am–10pm, Sun 9am–9pm; $

A quiet oasis removed from the bustle of Harvard Square. Indulge in an empty-calories meal of delectable handmade chocolates and pastries, accompanied by a great range of teas and coffees. Their hot chocolate is like a dessert in a cup.

⑤ THE RED HOUSE

98 Winthrop Street; tel: 617-576-0605; www.theredhouse. com; Tue–Sun noon–midnight, Fri–Sat until 1am; $$

In a quaint, red-painted clapboard house, dating from 1802, this charming restaurant with a large outdoor deck serves most of its mains in half-portions – great if you're not so hungry or on a budget.

LEXINGTON AND CONCORD

Following the 'Battle Road' between Lexington and Concord, west of Boston, will take you past key Revolutionary sites, as well as the beautiful landscape that inspired American literary giants.

Tourist Information

Lexington Visitor Center (1875 Massachusetts Avenue; tel: 781-862-1450; www. lexingtonchamber.org; daily Dec–Mar 10am–4pm, Apr–Nov 9am–5pm) is opposite Battle Green next to Buckman Tavern.

Revolution

The battles that started the American Revolution of 1775, leading up to the Declaration of Independence the following year, began in these neighboring villages, where the Minutemen – a militia of rebels against British rule – faced off against His Majesty's armies, the Redcoats.

DISTANCE 13 miles (20.5km) from Boston to Lexington; driving tour: 11 miles (18km)
TIME A full day
START National Heritage Museum, Lexington
END Walden Pond, Concord
POINTS TO NOTE

By car you can visit all the sites in a day. Spend the night in Concord if you would like to linger at any of the museums or historic houses or hike the Battle Road Trail. Many places are closed Sunday morning and from November to March.

If using public transportation, take bus 62 or 76 from Boston's Alewife T Station to Lexington center. From spring through fall, you can take the Liberty Ride tour *(see right)* between Lexington and Concord. Otherwise, try Yellow Cabs (tel: 781-862-4600). Commuter trains from Concord Depot take about 40 minutes to reach Boston's North Station.

Salem *(p.48)* is 23 miles (37km) east of Lexington.

LEXINGTON

To reach the start of this tour, drive out of Boston on Route 2. Turn right at exit 57 onto Route 4-225. As you approach the center of Lexington there are two sites of historical interest on the left.

National Heritage Museum

Begin at the **National Heritage Museum ❶** (tel: 781-861-6559; www. nationalheritagemuseum.org; Mon–Sat 10am–4.30pm, Sun noon–4.30pm;

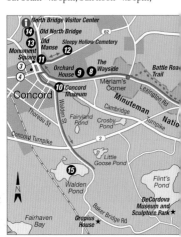

free), in a contemporary building entered on Marrett Road, which features changing exhibits of Americana across four centuries.

Soon after is the 1635 **Munroe Tavern ❷** (1332 Massachusetts Avenue; tel: 781-862-1703; www.lexingtonhistory.org; Apr–Oct daily noon–4pm, tours every hour; charge), which served as headquarters for the Redcoats and as a hospital on their retreat from Concord.

Battle Green

Drive into the center and park. At one corner of the town common, a tiny triangular park known as **Battle Green ❸**, stands the **Minuteman Statue**, honoring the 77 patriots who faced down the British here, igniting the American Revolution of 1775. They were called 'Minutemen' because they pledged to be ready to fight at a minute's notice.

Opposite on Bedford Street is **Buckman Tavern ❹** (1 Bedford Street; www.lexingtonhistory.org; Apr–Oct daily 10am–4pm, tours every half-hour; charge), a clapboard building that has been restored to its original late 17th-century appearance. After the first battle of the Revolution, wounded Minutemen were brought here for medical attention.

Hancock-Clarke House

A short walk northwest from Battle Green is **Hancock-Clarke House ❺** (36 Hancock Street; www.lexingtonhistory.org; Apr–Oct daily 10am–4pm, tours every hour; charge). Built in 1738, this house is where, on the night of April 18, 1771, Paul Revere woke John Hancock and Samuel Adams with the warning that the British were coming.

Above from far left:
clapboard Buckman Tavern; detail of the Minuteman statue on Battle Green.

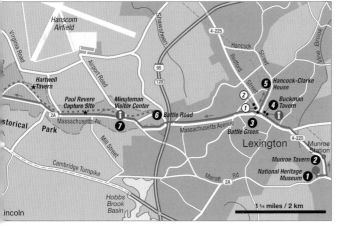

The Liberty Ride
On Saturday and Sunday from mid-April to early May and then daily until mid-October, the Liberty Ride (tel: 781-862-0500; www.liberty ride.us/libertyride.html) tour bus travels between Lexington and Concord visiting the key historic sites. It's a 90-minute continuous loop guided tour, and you can hop on and off as you please within a 48-hour period.

Before leaving Lexington you could get some refreshments at **Via Lago**, see ⑪①, facing Battle Green, or **Yangtze River**, see ⑪②, around the corner.

BATTLE ROAD

From Battle Green, drive east on Massachusetts Avenue to join Route 2A which shadows **Battle Road ❻**, along which the British, harried by the Minutemen, marched towards Concord. This whole area is preserved in the Minuteman National Historical Park, through which runs an easy 5-mile (8km) **walking trail** *(see dotted line on map)*. Stop off at the **Minuteman Visitor Center ❼** (tel: 978-369-6993; www.nps.gov/mima; Mar–Oct 9am–5pm, Nov until 4pm; free) to see an excellent multimedia presentation about the start of the Revolution.

CONCORD

The handsome small town of Concord is where the second engagement of the Revolution took place. During the first half of the 19th century a handful of renowned literati also lived here.

Literary Homes

On the way into Concord is **The Wayside ❽** (455 Lexington Road; tel: 978-318-7826; www.nps.gov/archive/mima/wayside; guided tours mid-May–Aug Wed–Sun, Sept–Oct Fri–Sun, phone ahead for tour times;

charge). Louisa May Alcott and her family lived here, as did Nathaniel Hawthorne in later years. Most of the furnishings, though, date from the residence of Margaret Sidney, the author of the *Five Little Peppers*.

Down the road is delightful **Orchard House ❾** (tel: 978-369-4118; www.louisamayalcott.org; Nov–Mar Mon–Fri 11am–3pm, Sat 10am–4.30pm, Sun 1–4.30pm, Apr–Oct Mon–Sat 10am–4.30pm, Sun 1–4.30pm; charge), the Alcott family home from 1858 to 1877, where Louisa May wrote *Little Women* and her father, Bronson, founded his school of philosophy.

Concord Museum

Where Lexington Road meets the Cambridge Turnpike (Route 2) is the splendid **Concord Museum ❿** (tel: 978-369-9763; www.concordmuseum.org; Mon–Sat 9am–5pm, Sun noon–5pm; charge). It contains one of the two lanterns that were hung in Boston's Old North Church to warn patriots that the Redcoats were leaving for Concord and Lexington. Here, too, you can see Ralph Waldo Emerson's study, which was transferred from the wooden Emerson House across the road. There are also artifacts associated with the author Henry Thoreau, including the writing desk from his Walden Pond abode.

Monument Square

Around ¼ mile (400m) farther west is **Monument Square ⓫**, the heart of

---

Walden Pond

Drive south out of Concord along Walden Street, which crosses Route 2, for 1½ miles (2.5km) to find Walden Pond (parking charge), which inspired Thoreau's memoir *Walden* (1854). It takes about an hour to circle the relatively small pond on foot. The best time to visit is in the fall. During summer the pond is a popular swimming spot. A cairn of stones stands alongside the site where the writer lived in a cabin between 1845 and 1847.

Concord. On the square's east side is **The Colonial Inn**, see ⑪③.

Park your car, and from the square stroll east along Bedford Street (Route 62) to reach **Sleepy Hollow Cemetery** ⑫. In an idyllic setting in the northeast corner of the cemetery lies Authors' Ridge, the resting place of Hawthorne, the Alcotts, Emerson and Thoreau.

Old Manse

Return to Monument Square and drive north for about a mile (nearly 2km) on Monument Street to arrive at the **Old Manse** ⑬ (tel: 978-369-3909; www.thetrustees.org; mid-Apr–Oct Mon–Sat 10am–5pm, Sun noon–5pm; charge), set in immaculate grounds (free to visit). It was from this 1770 building that the Rev. William Emerson watched the battle in 1775 for the nearby Old North Bridge. It was later the residence of his grandson, Ralph Waldo Emerson, and then the Hawthornes.

Old North Bridge

From the Old Manse, walk to the replica **Old North Bridge** ⑭ across the Concord River. On the other side stands the **Minuteman statue**, rifle in one hand, ploughshare in the other. Emerson's immortal words 'The shot heard 'round the world' are inscribed on the plinth. On a hill overlooking the bridge is the **North Bridge Visitor Center** (tel: 978-369-6993; daily 9am–5pm).

Return to the center of Concord to find **Main Streets Market and Café**, see ⑪④. If you are travelling by public transportation, Concord Depot MBTA commuter rail station is a short walk west on Thoreau Street. If driving, you could make a detour to **Walden Pond** ⑮ *(see margin, left)*.

Food and Drink

① VIA LAGO
1845 Massachusetts Avenue, Lexington; tel: 781-861-8276; www.vialagocatering.com; Mon–Wed 7am–9pm, Thur–Sat 7am–9.30pm; $
Freshly made sandwiches, light meals, and other snacks are available from this convivial café within sight of Battle Green.

② YANGTZE RIVER
25 Depot Square, Lexington; tel: 781-861-6030; www.yangtzelexington.com; daily 11.30am–9.15pm, Fri–Sat until 10.15pm; $
Lexington has a large Chinese population, and the fact that many of them frequent this restaurant proves how good the food is. The dim sum and all-you-can-eat buffet brunch at the weekend are a steal.

③ THE COLONIAL INN
48 Monument Square, Concord; tel: 978-369-9200; www.concordscolonialinn.com; daily 7am–9pm; $$
Dating back to 1716, this is as traditional as it gets in Concord, although all but 12 of the hotel's 60 rooms are in a modern brick annexe. Meals are available throughout the day, but book at least 24 hours in advance for their formal high tea, served Fri–Sun 3–5pm.

④ MAIN STREETS MARKET AND CAFÉ
42 Main Street, Concord; tel: 978-369-9948; www.mainstreetsmarketandcafe.com; Sun–Mon 7am–5.30pm, Tue–Thur 7am–10pm, Fri–Sat 7am–11pm; $
A bustling self-serve hangout during the day, when it is probably best to grab a delicious cake and coffee to enjoy down at Walden Pond. There is live music here most evenings.

SALEM AND CAPE ANN

Stroll around Salem, one of New England's most historic towns, then use it as a base for exploring the rugged coves, fishing towns, artists' colonies, and grand New England mansions of Cape Ann.

DISTANCE Salem to Rockport: 23½ miles (38km); walking tour in Salem: 3½ miles (5.5km)
TIME Two days
START Salem
END Rockport
POINTS TO NOTE

Salem is 16 miles (26km) north of Boston. Driving is the best way of getting around Cape Ann; the scenic coastal route follows MA 127 beyond Salem. However, Salem, Gloucester, and Rockport can all be reached by train from Boston's North Station (see www.mbta.com). There's also a ferry that connects Salem and Boston from May to October (tel: 978-741-0220; www.salemferry.com; one way/round trip $13/24; 45 minutes), and you can get around on Cape Ann Transportation Authority buses (www.canntran.com).

Tourist Information
In Salem, the National Park Visitor Center (just off Essex Mall on New Liberty Street; tel: 978-740-1650; www.nps.gov; daily 9am–5pm) is the place to pick up maps and leaflets, consult the park rangers, and watch an excellent 25-minute film about the county's history. You can also find useful information at www.salem.org.

For more about Cape Ann, try www.seecapeann.com, www.capeannvacations.com, and www.rockportusa.com.

SALEM

Once one of the nation's great seaports, Salem produced the country's first millionaires, and has the architectural and cultural heritage to prove it in its McIntire Historic District and the protected properties of the Peabody Essex Museum. However, it does not take long to find reminders of the activities most often associated with the town – the trials and executions of 'witches.'

Witch Dungeon Museum

Park your car near **Salem Station** and walk down Washington Street, turning right onto Lynde Street after two blocks. At no. 16 is the **Witch Dungeon Museum ❶** (tel: 978-741-3570; www.witchdungeon.com; daily 10am–5pm; charge), where you can watch a vividly staged reenactment of a trial, adapted from a 1692 manuscript, before being guided through the tiny dank dungeons in which the accused were held.

Witch House

The spooky wooden house on the corner of Essex and North streets is the **Witch House ❷** (tel: 978-744-8815; mid-May–Nov daily 10am–5pm; charge), where trial magistrate Jonathan Corwin cross-examined more than 200 suspected witches; the decor is authentic to the period.

McIntire Historic District

Named for Samuel McIntire (1757–1811), one of the foremost American architects of his day, this historic area of Salem, roughly bounded by Federal, Flint, Broad, and Summer/North Streets, showcases four centuries of architectural styles.

Backtrack from the Witch House to Federal Street, where at no. 80 stands the McIntire-designed **Peirce-Nichols House ❸** (*c.*1782); its east parlor has been restored and is open for tours by arrangement with the Peabody Essex Museum *(see p.50)*.

Return to Essex Street and proceed to no. 318, the Georgian-period **Ropes Mansion ❹**, which stands in a beautiful garden and features a rare collection of Nanking porcelain and Irish glass.

Turn into quaint Botts Court and walk to Chestnut Street, one of Salem's finest thoroughfares. At no. 34 is the fine **Phillips House ❺** (tel: 978-744-0440; www.historicnewengland.org; 11am–4pm June–Oct Tue–Sun, Nov–

May Sat–Sun, tours every half-hour; charge), where the carriage house contains several antique cars. Retrace your steps back along Chestnut Street, and continue to no. 9, the red-brick Federalist gem **Hamilton Hall ❻** (tel: 978-744-0805; www.hamiltonhall.org; Mon–Fri 9am–3pm; free).

Refreshment Option

From the corner of Chestnut Street, turn left onto Summer Street and then right at Essex Street to reach the pedestrian Essex Mall, recognizable by the red paving that matches the red bricks of the buildings. Turn right onto Central Street to find **Red's Sandwich Shop**, see ⑪①.

Above from far left: replica of the *Friendship* at Derby Wharf; House of the Seven Gables.

Food and Drink

① RED'S SANDWICH SHOP
15 Central Street; tel: 978-745-3257; www.redssandwich shop.com; Mon–Sat 5am–3pm, Sun 6am–1pm; $
A Salem breakfast institution housed in the old London Coffee House, dating from 1698. Arrive early if you don't want to stand in line.

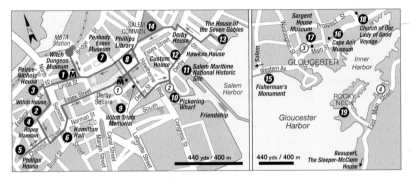

Peabody Essex Museum

Back on the mall, reserve a decent block of time to visit the outstanding **Peabody Essex Museum** ❼ (tel: 978-745-9500; http://pem.org; daily 10am–5pm; charge), where an impressive contemporary building by Moshe Safdie displays a fraction of the collection of nearly a million objects.

The museum's origins date back to 1799 and to the art and antiques amassed by Salem's seafaring merchants on their global travels. Ships' models, figureheads, nautical instruments, charts and maps abound, but the museum also has fine antiques from China, Japan and India, as well as plenty of artifacts from the South Pacific (especially the Solomon Islands) and further afield. There's also a 200-year-old Chinese merchant's home, transported from China and rebuilt as part of the museum; entry to this is by timed ticket and advance reservations are advised.

Phillips Library

Diagonally opposite the Peabody Essex Museum, a mini architectural park surrounds the red-brick **Phillips Library** ❽ (tel: 978-745-9500; http://pem.org; Wed 10am–5pm, Thur 1–5pm; free), which has a lovely reading room. Notice the stark contrast between the massive columns of the **Andrew-Safford House** (1819; 13 Washington Square) and, behind it, the tiny features of the **Derby-Beebe Summerhouse** (1799). Also here are the **Gardner-Pingree House** (1804; 128 Essex Street) and, from 1727, the neighboring **Crowninshield-Bentley House**.

Witch Trials Memorial

On leaving the Peabody, follow the short footpath around its side until you reach Charter Street. Here, next to the Burying Point Cemetery – resting place of witch judge John Hathorne – is the most poignant of all Salem's witch-connected sites. The **Witch Trials Memorial** ❾, dedi-

---

Food and Drink

② **FINZ**

76 Wharf Street; tel: 978-744-8485; www.hipfinz.com/salem.php; daily 11.30am–midnight; $–$$

The best place to enjoy seafood overlooking Salem Harbor. Bypass the tasteless lobster roll in favor of the excellent salmon wrap or great-value haddock sandwich.

Salem's Witch Hysteria

In 1692, between June and September, Salem fell under the dark spell of mass hysteria and executed 14 women and six men for witchcraft. You would be forgiven for thinking that the town is still obsessed with witches, for that sad history, portrayed in the Arthur Miller play *The Crucible*, is recalled at many sites – a few historical, others mostly kitsch. Every October the town ramps up its black-arts connection even more to run a month-long celebration called Haunted Happenings (www.hauntedhappenings.org), culminating in the crowning of the king and queen of Halloween on the 31st.

cated by Holocaust survivor and renowned writer Elie Wiesel in 1992, is a contemplative space surrounded by 20 stone benches etched with the trial victims' names, and shaded by a clump of black locust trees – reputedly the kind from which the convicted were hanged.

Salem Maritime National Historic Site

From the cemetery, cross Derby Street and walk along its south side toward **Pickering Wharf ⑩**, a touristy collection of stores and restaurants including several antiques shops. The best place to eat around here is **Finz**, see ⑪②.

Next to the wharf, the **Salem Maritime National Historic Site ⑪** focuses on Salem's port. Stop by the **Orientation Center** (tel: 978-740-1660; www.nps.gov; daily 9am–5pm) to find out about ranger-guided tours (charge) to the nearby Custom House, Derby House, and Narbonne House, as well as the *Friendship*, a full-scale replica of a 1797 three-masted East India merchant ship. It is docked at Derby Wharf, which is one of the few wharves that remain from the 40 of Salem's heyday.

Custom House

Facing the wharf is the **Custom House ⑫** (1819), surmounted by a gilded eagle clutching arrows and a shield in its claws, which was made

famous by Nathaniel Hawthorne. Salem's most famous son worked here for three years of 'slavery,' on which he based the introduction of *The Scarlet Letter* (1850).

Adjacent to the Custom House is the **Hawkes House** (1780; not open to the public) and, beyond that, the ochre-brick **Derby House** (1761). The former was built by shipowner Elias Hasket Derby (probably America's first millionaire) to replace the latter, but it was never completed and was used as a storehouse for booty taken by his Revolutionary privateers.

The House of the Seven Gables

Continue down Derby Street from the Custom House to reach, at no. 115, **The House of the Seven Gables ⑬** (tel: 978-744-0991; www.7gables.org; daily July–Oct 10am–7pm, mid-Jan–June and Nov–Dec 10am–5pm; charge), which inspired Hawthorne to write the 1851 novel of the same name. The small house in which he was born in 1806 has been moved into the grounds. Guides will lead you through rooms stuffed with period furniture. Take a breather in the lovely garden afterwards.

Return to the town center by walking via **Salem Common ⑭**, where you will find the historic **Hawthorne Hotel** *(see p.108)*, an ideal base for the night. You could have a meal at the **Lyceum** on Church Street *(see p.116).*

Above from far left: Custom House; the Peabody Essex Museum displays all kinds of maritime artifacts.

Below: figureheads in the Peabody Essex.

GLOUCESTER

Take the coastal route MA 127 north-east out of Salem and continue on for 16 miles (26km) to **Gloucester**. Founded in 1623, it is the nation's oldest seaport. Unlike Salem, its harbor is still fairly active (although not as busy as it used to be), with many fishermen now of Portuguese or Italian descent.

On the way into town, just over the drawbridge spanning the Annisquam Canal stands the **Fisherman's Monument** 🄵, depicting a helmsman gripping a wheel as he scans the horizon. Those familiar with the book and film *The Perfect Storm*, about an ill-fated Gloucester crew, will know that the poignancy of this memorial to those who have perished at sea is not merely a matter of ancient history.

Town Walk

Begin an exploration of the town at the **Cape Ann Museum** 🄶 (27 Pleasant Street; tel: 978-283-0455; www.capeann museum.org; Tue–Sat 10am–5pm, Sun 1–4pm; charge), displaying seascapes by the renowned American maritime painter Fitz Hugh Lane, and an inter-esting collection of furniture, silver, and porcelain, in the handsome home of Captain Elias Davis (1804) and the adjoining White-Ellery House (*c.*1709).

The **Sargent House Museum** 🄷 (tel: 978-281-2432; mid-May–mid-Oct Fri–Sun noon–last tour at 3pm; charge) is a short walk west along Middle Street at no. 49. The home of Judith Sargent Murray, an early advo-cate of women's rights, recreates the decor of 1782 when the house was built. A block south, toward the harbor, you will find several lunch options on Main Street, including **Passports**, see ⑪③.

Below: Rockport.

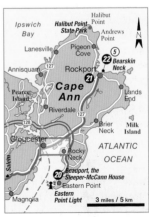

Above from far left: Gloucester harbor at dusk; colorful fishing floats.

Walk east on Main Street for 500m/ yds and turn left on Prospect Street for the attractive Portuguese **Church of Our Lady of Good Voyage** , recognizable by its two blue cupolas.

Rocky Neck and Eastern Point

Now drive around the harbor to East Main Street, passing **Duckworth's Bistrot**, see ⑪④, and heading on to **Rocky Neck** ⑲ (www.rockyneckart colony.org), the oldest artists' colony in the US, in a wonderful coastal setting. Rudyard Kipling worked on *Captains Courageous* (1897), about Gloucester fishermen, while staying here.

On leaving Rocky Neck, turn right onto Eastern Point Road. After about 1 mile (1.5km), take the right fork, even though it's marked 'private.' This is the exclusive enclave of Eastern Point, which has a score of magnificent homes. Open to the public is **Beauport, the Sleeper-McCann House** ⑳ (tel: 978-283-0800; www.historicnewengland. org; June–mid-Oct Tue–Sat 10am–last tour at 4pm; charge), which was built and furnished between 1907 and 1934 by Henry Davis Sleeper, a collector of American art and antiquities. On the tour you can see rooms he decorated to cover different periods of American life.

ROCKPORT

About 7 miles (11km) northeast of Gloucester is picturesque **Rockport** ㉑, once a shipping center for locally cut granite. In the 1920s Rockport was discovered by artists and it remains an art colony today. A dozen or so galleries display works of both local and international artists on Main Street, but what attracts most tourists is **Bearskin Neck** ㉒. This narrow peninsula, jutting out beyond the harbor, is densely packed with tiny dwellings and old fishing sheds, now converted into galleries, antiques stores, and restaurants.

Enjoy magnificent views of the Atlantic from the breakwater at the end of the Neck, just before which you will pass **My Place by the Sea**, see ⑪⑤.

Food and Drink

③ PASSPORTS
110 Main Street, Gloucester; tel: 978-281-3680; Mon–Fri 11.30am–9pm, Sat 11.30am–10pm, Sun noon–9.30pm; $
Ideal for lunch or a quick snack, this romantically themed café has local artwork covering the walls and does great salads, soups, and seafood.

④ DUCKWORTH'S BISTROT
197 East Main Street, Gloucester; tel: 978-282-4426; www.duckworthsbistrot.com; Tue–Sun 5–9.30pm; $$
A great place to return for dinner after a day's outing around Cape Ann. Chef Ken Duckworth's modern American cuisine uses the best of local produce. Many dishes, such as grilled organic chicken and sautéed veal cutlets, also come in half-portions.

⑤ MY PLACE BY THE SEA
68 Bearskin Neck, Rockport; tel: 978-546-9667; www.my placebythesea.com; May–early Dec daily 11.30am–3pm, 5–9pm; $$
Fantastic views are guaranteed at this friendly place that serves imaginative modern American cuisine. It is good value for lunch, but pricier for dinner, when reservations are advised.

SOUTH SHORE AND CAPE COD

This road trip down the shoreline along which New England was founded links historic Plymouth with laid-back Provincetown at the tip of Cape Cod via pretty coastal villages and national park-protected dunes and beaches.

Tourist Information

In Plymouth, at the Waterfront Tourist Information Center (170 Water Street; tel: 508-747-7533; www. visit-plymouth.com; Apr–Nov 9am–5pm, June–Aug 9am–8pm) you can rent an MP3 player for a guided walk around the town (also downloadable from their website).

In Provincetown, head to the Chamber of Commerce (tel: 508-487-3424; www. ptownchamber.com; Jan–Mar Mon and Fri 11am–3pm, Apr–May, Nov–Dec Mon–Sat 10.30am–5pm, June–Oct daily 9am– 6.30pm) at the foot of MacMillan Wharf. See also www.province town.com.

DISTANCE 78 miles (125km)
TIME Two to three days
START Plymouth
END Provincetown
POINTS TO NOTE

Plymouth is a 40-mile (64km) drive south of Boston along I-93, then Route 3. There are direct MBTA trains to Plymouth, but the service is limited and the station is about 2 miles (3km) from the town center. Instead, take one of the more frequent trains to Kingston, from where Gatra buses (tel: 1-800-483-2500; www.gatra.org) run to Plymouth's center. Alternatively, Plymouth and Brockton buses (tel: 508-746-0373; www.p-b.com) run from Boston to Plymouth's bus depot, just off Route 3, around 2 miles (3km) southwest of Plymouth Rock; they also offer services to Provincetown via Hyannis. Many places in Provincetown are closed mid-Dec–mid-Mar. Providence *(see p.64)* is 42.5 miles (68km) west of Plymouth on Route 44.

Despite all the fuss made over Plymouth Rock, history relates that Plymouth was not the Pilgrim Fathers' first landfall in the New World. That honor belongs to Provincetown at the tip of Cape Cod, where a small party landed on November 21, 1620. Walking tours around these two historic towns bookend a road trip that passes through other attractive pit stops along the cape.

PLYMOUTH

Park near the **Waterfront Tourist Information Center** *(see margin, left)*, and walk south along Water Street towards **Pilgrim Memorial State Park**. Its focus is **Plymouth Rock ❶**, identified in 1741 by a third-generation elder of the Plymouth Church as the rock on which the Pilgrim Fathers first stepped, in December 1620, on reaching America.

Mayflower II

Nearby is the ***Mayflower II ❷*** (tel: 508-746-1622; www.plimoth.org; Apr–Nov daily 9am–5pm; charge), a replica of the original *Mayflower*, built in England and sailed to Plymouth in 1957. The

vessel vividly conveys the hardships that the 102 members of the crew suffered during the original 55-day voyage.

Beside the Town Brook

Follow Water Street south to **Brewster Gardens** ❸, which hugs both sides of the **Town Brook** from which the first Native Americans and, later, the British settlers got their fresh water and herring.

Cross the wooden bridge and follow the brook under two road bridges to arrive at **Jenney Grist Mill** ❹ (6 Spring Lane; tel: 508-747-4544; www.jenney gristmill.org; Apr–mid-Nov Wed–Mon 9.30am–4.30pm; charge), located on the site of the mill established in 1636 by John Jenney. Corn is still ground here as it was in the Pilgrims' time.

Turn right off Spring Lane onto Summer Street to find, at no. 42, the oldest home in Plymouth. The **Richard Sparrow House** ❺ (tel: 508-747-1240; www.sparrowhouse.com; Apr–Dec Thur–Tue 10am–5pm; charge) dates from 1640 and is set up so you can see how the early settlers lived.

Mayflower Society House

Follow Summer Street, turn left on Market Street and walk through the Town Square to Main Street, Plymouth's central shopping street, where you will find **Kiskadee Coffee Company**, see ①①. Take the second right onto North Street, along which is the whitewashed 1754 **Mayflower Society House** ❻ (tel: 508-746-2590; www.the

mayflowersociety.com; July–Aug daily 11am–4pm, June and Sept–Oct Fri–Sun only; charge). Tours of the interior reflect the occupants down the centuries, while behind the house is a library for genealogical research.

Above from far left: quiet Cape Cod village; *Mayflower II* at Plymouth; empty dunes on the cape's seashore.

Food and Drink

① KISKADEE COFFEE COMPANY
18 Main Street; tel: 508-830-1410; www.kiskadee coffee.com; Mon–Fri 6.30am–6pm, Thur until 8.30pm, Sat–Sun 7.30am–6pm; $
They do coffee, of course, but also a big range of bagel and panini sandwiches as well as other tempting freshly baked goods. Free internet is also a plus.

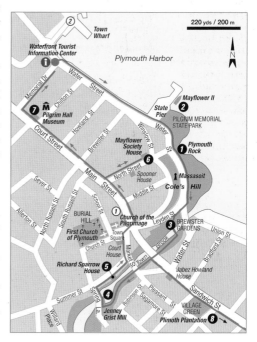

Pilgrim Hall Museum

Return to Main Street and continue north along Court Street to the 1824 **Pilgrim Hall Museum** ❼ (tel: 508-746-1620; www.pilgrimhall.org; Feb–Dec daily 9am–4.30pm; charge), which features an extensive collection of memorabilia from the first Pilgrim families, a range of Native American artifacts and the remains of *Sparrow Hawk*, a sailing ship that was wrecked in 1626.

Turn right down Memorial Drive to arrive back at the Tourist Information Center. Across the road is the Town Wharf and **Lobster Hut**, see ❶②.

PLIMOTH PLANTATION

It is 2½ miles (4km) southeast from the center of Plymouth to the **Plimoth Plantation** ❽ (137 Warren Avenue; tel: 508-746-1622; www.plimoth.org; Apr–Nov daily 9am–5pm; charge), where the year is always 1627; they use the 17th-century phonetic spelling for Plymouth, as Governor William Bradford did in his diary. In the plantation's English Village actor-guides dressed in authentic 17th-century costumes and speaking in old English dialects portray historical residents of the colony, salting fish, shearing sheep, and baking bread in clay ovens. The **Wampanoag Homesite** shows how Native Americans lived in Massachusetts in the 1620s, and is a rare chance to meet native people in traditional dress and find out about their ancient culture and skills.

UPPER CAPE

Around 15 miles (24km) south of Plymouth, Route 3 crosses the Cape Cod Canal via the Sagamore Bridge. From here, follow the old King's Highway (Route 6A) which hugs the western coastline of the Upper Cape as it winds its way through a series of pretty villages.

Sandwich

The first major one you will come to is **Sandwich** ❾, where **The Dan'l Webster Inn** offers comfortable lodgings *(see p.108)*. The **Sandwich Glass Museum** (129 Main Street; tel: 508-888-0251; www.sandwichglassmuseum.org; Apr–Dec 9.30am–5pm, Feb–Mar Wed–Sun 9.30am–4pm; charge) celebrates the town's 19th-century glassmaking history with rooms of colored glassware as well as glassblowing demonstrations.

Head south on Grove Street to find the **Heritage Museums and Gardens** (tel: 508-888-3300; www.heritagemuseumsandgardens.org; Apr–Oct daily 10am–5pm, Nov–Dec Wed–Sun 10am–4pm; charge). There is something for everyone in its beautifully

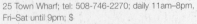

Food and Drink

② LOBSTER HUT

25 Town Wharf; tel: 508-746-2270; daily 11am–8pm, Fri–Sat until 9pm; $

Really nothing fancy, but when it comes to enjoying seafood within toe-dipping distance of the water then this Plymouth institution is the place to head to.

landscaped 100-acre (40ha) grounds, with galleries showing folk art, militaria, and old automobiles, plus a working carousel from 1912 that kids will adore.

Yarmouth and Brewster

The flavor of this unspoiled corner of the cape is typified in **Yarmouth Port** ❿, 15 miles (24km) east of Sandwich, where the handsome 1840 Greek Revival **Captain Bangs Hallett House** (11 Strawberry Lane; tel: 508-362-3021; www.hsoy.org/historic/hallet house.htm; June–Oct Thur–Sun tours

at 1, 2 and 3pm; charge) has its parlours arranged as if the captain was just back from a voyage to China; out back, nature trails crisscross 50 acres (20ha) of meadow and woods.

At **Brewster** ⓫, 12 miles (19km) farther east, there are more trails to explore at the **Cape Cod Museum of Natural History** (869 Main Street; tel: 508-896-3867; www.ccmnh.org; 11am–3pm Feb–Mar Thur–Sun, Apr–May and Oct–Dec Wed–Sun, June–Sept daily 9.30am–4pm; charge), as well as exhibits about the cape's flora and fauna.

Above from far left:
Native American dress at the Wampanoag Homesite; glassblowing at Sandwich; 1627 English Village at the Plimoth Plantation.

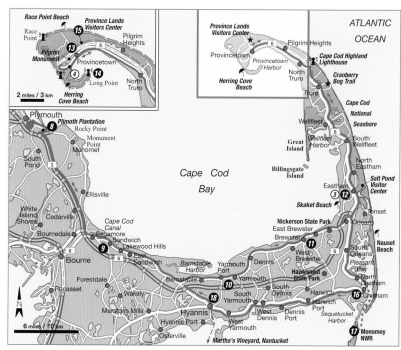

Above from left:
Provincetown Art Association & Museum; Chatham's Old Godfrey Windmill; Race Point Beach.

LOWER CAPE

The confusingly named 'Lower Cape,' the outer part, begins at **Orleans**, 5 miles (8km) past Brewster. Not far from the town's busy traffic circle are two fine beaches – **Nauset** (Beach Road) on the colder, rougher Atlantic ocean side, and **Skaket** (Skaket Beach Road), which has calm bay frontage.

Follow Route 6 for 3 miles (5km) north to **Eastham** ⑫, home to the lobster shack **Arnold's**, see ⑪③, and the **Cape Cod National Seashore's Salt Pond Visitor Center** (Doane Road; tel: 508-255-3421; daily 9am–4.30pm), with exhibits about the dune lands that stretch north for 30 miles (48km) along the Great Beach to Provincetown, 19 miles (31km) farther along Route 6.

Ferries to P-Town
From May to October several daily ferries run between Boston and Provincetown, taking 1½ hours one-way; see www.boston harborcruises.com and www.baystate cruisecompany.com for details.

PROVINCETOWN

Thick with antiques, crafts and souvenir shops, art galleries, cafés, restaurants, and bars, **Provincetown** ⑬, or 'P-town,' is an unashamed tourist destination, but also, thanks to strict town ordinances, a beautiful-looking one. It's no surprise that generations of artists have been drawn to P-town and continue to practice here. There is also a lively gay scene.

The East End

Entering P-town along the one-way Commercial Street from the south, you will first hit the **East End**, packed with galleries as well as, at no. 460, the **Provincetown Art Association & Museum** (PAAM; tel: 508-487-1750; www.paam.org; May–Sept Mon–Thur 11am–8pm, Fri 11am–10pm, Sat–Sun 11am–5pm; Oct–May Thur–Sun noon–5pm; charge). Top-class exhibitions are staged here, maintaining a tradition that started in 1899 with the founding of the Cape Cod School of Art by Charles Hawthorne.

Pilgrim Monument

The Pilgrim Fathers anchored in Provincetown before heading off to Plymouth, an event commemorated by the 252ft (77m) **Pilgrim Monument and Provincetown Museum** (High Pole Hill Road; tel: 508-487-1310; www.pilgrim-monument.org; daily Apr–May and mid-Sept–Nov 9am–5pm, June–mid-Sept 9am–7pm;

Food and Drink

③ ARNOLD'S
3580 State Highway/Route 6, Eastham; tel: 508-255-2575; www.arnoldsrestaurant.com; May–mid-June Fri–Sun 11.30am–8pm, mid-June–Oct daily 11.30am–9.30pm; $–$$
A long-running lobster and clam bar that also serves award-winning ice cream and has a fun mini-golf course to entertain the kids.

④ RED INN
15 Commercial Street, Provincetown; tel: 508-487-7334; www.theredinn.com; May–Oct daily 5.30pm–late, Fri–Sun 11.30am–3pm, rest of year Sat–Sun dinner only; $$$
One of the most pleasant places to dine in P-town is this elegant West End inn, with beautiful gardens and a prime beachside position. The cuisine is modern American and the portions are generous. There is also accommodation here, if you decide to stay over.

charge). To get your bearings of P-town's confusing geography, and for a grand 360-degree view of the Lower Cape, it is worth slogging up the tower's 116 steps and 60 ramps.

The West End

Farther down Commercial Street past a smattering of antiques shops, follow the road left around the Coast Guard Station to the **West End** of town, where weatherboard guesthouses and private residences are surrounded by lovely flower gardens. Particularly picturesque is the aptly named **Red Inn**, see ⑪④, on the lawns of which you will often see art classes being held.

Cape Cod National Seashore

Provincetown's best beaches are part of the **Cape Cod National Seashore** (CCNS), which includes **Long Point** ⓮, the slender sandbar that hooks back into Cape Cod Bay. You can reach here by walking across the breakwater at the far west end of Commercial Street; the uneven stones can make the crossing a challenge. Once on Long Point you can aim either right to the lighthouse at Wood End or left to the lighthouse on the tip of the sandbar – going in this direction you will pass the P-town nudist beach.

North along the coast towards the Atlantic side of the Cape, **Herring Cove Beach** is popular with families and a fine spot to watch sunsets. Farther around, and pinpointed by another lighthouse, is **Race Point Beach**, behind which is P-town's airport.

A fine view of the area can be had from the observation deck above the **Province Lands Visitors Center** ⓯ (tel: 508-487-1256; www.nps.gov/caco; May–Oct daily 9am–5pm; free), where you can find out about ranger-led walks around the national park. Note if you bring your car or bike into the national park area there is a small charge.

RETURN TO UPPER CAPE

As you journey towards Boston or head on to Providence *(see p.64)*, check out the Atlantic Coast side of the cape. From Orleans, continue south for 7 miles (11km) on Route 28 to upscale **Chatham** ⓰, where you watch the fishing fleet return to the Fish Pier in the late afternoon, or take a boat ride to the 2,700-acre (6,670ha) **Monomoy National Wildlife Refuge** ⓱ (tel: 508-945-0594; www.fws.gov/northeast/monomoy), a haven for birds and seals.

Hyannis

Route 28 back to the mainland passes through the busiest and most developed part of the cape. The main stop along this stretch is **Hyannis** ⓲ (19 miles/31km west of Chatham), which is famous as the summer residence of the Kennedy family. Here you can catch a ferry to **Martha's Vineyard** or **Nantucket** (tel: 800-492-8082; www. hy-linecruises.com; *see also margin*).

Martha's Vineyard and Nantucket

Martha's Vineyard's hills, meadows, and country lanes are perfect for cyclists. Edgartown has a number of sea captains' homes converted into upscale inns, while Oak Bluffs is more of a family resort; Vineyard Haven is the main commercial center.

Nantucket, 30 miles (48km) out to sea, was a whalers' haven in the 19th-century era of *Moby-Dick*. Its only real town, Nantucket, reflects those days in its cobblestoned streets and brick mansions. The island's windswept moorland is surrounded by breathtaking expanses of ocean beach.

For details, see www.marthas-vineyard.com and www.mvy.com, or www.nantucketchamber.org and www.islandofnantucket.info.

THE BERKSHIRES AND PIONEER VALLEY

Towns such as Stockbridge, Lenox, and North Adams in the gently rolling hills of west Massachusetts are among the venues for art galleries, renowned summer music festivals, and the splendor of fall foliage.

DISTANCE 184 miles (296km)
TIME Two to three days
START/END Springfield
POINTS TO NOTE

Springfield is 90 miles (145km) west of Boston and connected to it by Amtrak trains. From Springfield it is 65 miles (105km) south to New Haven *(see p.68)* and 60 miles (97km) north to Brattleboro *(see p.72)*. See www.berkshires.org for more on the Berkshires and www.valleyvisitor.com for Pioneer Valley.

While Massachusetts's Berkshire Hills are far less rugged than the mountains of Vermont and New Hampshire, they do incorporate a refreshing variety of scenery. Benefiting from their proximity to Boston and New York, the hills have long been a favorite countryside escape for urbanites and artists, such as Norman Rockwell, who made Stockbridge his home in his latter years. The area has also become famous for its summer roster of high-profile arts festivals *(see p.23)*.

Food and Drink 🍴

① **CAFÉ LEBANON**
1390 Main Street, Springfield; tel: 413-737-7373; www.cafelebanon.com; Mon–Thur 11.30am–9pm, Fri until 10pm, Sat 3–10pm; $$
All the Middle Eastern favorites are served at this casual eatery, which spices things up with belly-dancing on Friday and Saturday nights.

SPRINGFIELD

The **Pioneer Valley**, named for the 17th-century settlers of the area, forms the eastern gateway to the region, where the largest city is **Springfield ❶**.

Begin in the reasonably handsome and busy downtown area by exploring the five institutions that make up **Springfield Museums** (21 Edwards Street; tel: 413-263-6800; www.springfieldmuseums.org; Tue–Sun 11am–4pm; charge). The **Connecticut Valley Historical Museum** focuses on local history; the **George Walter Vincent Smith Art Museum** is strong in Japanese art, armor, and decorative items; the **Michele & Donald D'Amour Museum of Fine Arts** exhibits American

Above from far left:
Ashley House in
Historic Deerfield;
walking in the Berk-
shires; Springfield
Armory National
Historic Site.

and French Impressionist works; the **Springfield Science Museum** (Tue–Sat 10am–5pm, Sun 11am–5pm) has inter-active displays; and the new **Museum of Springfield History** looks at the city's development as a manufacturing center. In the Quadrangle, bronze sculptures of beloved characters make up the delight-ful **Dr Seuss Sculpture Garden** (www.catinthehat.org; free), honoring the city's famous children's book writer. A short walk south of the museums is **Café Lebanon**, see ⑪①.

Armory and Basketball Museums

Due to its location on the conve-niently navigable Connecticut River, Springfield was selected as the site of the first US arsenal. Ten minutes' walk north of the Springfield Museums is the **Springfield Armory National Historic Site** (1 Armory Square; tel: 413-734-8551; www.nps.gov/spar; daily 9am–5pm; free), which tells the story of nearly 200 years of armament manufacturing.

Beside the Riverfront Park is the state-of-the-art **Naismith Memorial Basketball Hall of Fame** (1000 West Columbus Avenue; tel: 413-781-6500; www.hoophall.com; Mon–Sat 10am–5pm, Sun 10am–4pm; charge), named for Dr James Naismith, who invented the sport in 1891 in Springfield.

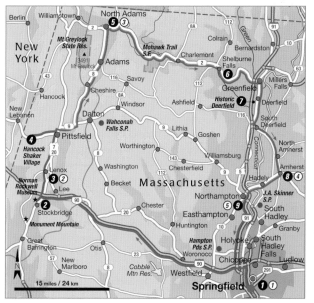

Great Barrington
Come summer both Lenox and Stock-bridge can get pretty busy with the various arts festivals going on. If you are stuck for somewhere to stay, try Great Barrington, 13 miles (21km) south of Lenox along Route 7. This arty town, with boutiques, antiques shops, restaurants, and cafés, can be used as a base for short hikes at Barth-olomew's Cobble (Route 7A; www.the trustees.org), a rocky riverside glade, or up Monument Mountain (Route 7; www.berk shirehiking.com).

Above from left:
Norman Rockwell's
studio near Stock-
bridge; Bridge
of Flowers at
Shelburne Falls.

MASS MoCA
One of the state's
best art museums,
MASS MoCA,
occupies a vast,
renovated 19th-
century factory
complex. Its fine
collection of contem-
porary art, including
giant pieces by the
likes of Sol Le Witt
and Anselm Kiefer, is
displayed across 19
light-filled galleries,
including one as large
as a football field.
Within the complex
you will also find a
performance arts
center, presenting a
year-round program
of dance, cabaret,
films, and avant-
garde theatre, and
Kidspace, a contem-
porary art gallery and
workshop devoted
to youngsters.

THE BERKSHIRES

Stockbridge

Follow I-90 west from Springfield for
48 miles (77km) to **Stockbridge ❷**,
where the artist Norman Rockwell
(1894–1978), chronicler of American
life, lived for 25 years. Main Street
looks much as it did when Rockwell
painted it back in the 1960s, save for
the weird and wonderful outsized
sculptures that dot the town in a festival held each year from June to the
end of October. The historic **Red Lion
Inn** *(see p.109)* on Main Street is a
good place to eat and stay.

To see original paintings by Rockwell
– far more vivid than the magazine
covers they became – and his charming
studio, drive 2 miles (3km) west to the
Norman Rockwell Museum (9 Glen-
dale Road, Route 183; tel: 413-298-
4100; www.nrm.org; May–Oct daily
10am–5pm, Nov–Apr Mon–Fri 10am–
4pm, Sat–Sun 10am–5pm; charge).

The other estate worth seeing in the
area is that of the sculptor Daniel
Chester French, who created the Lincoln Memorial in Washington DC and
the Minuteman statue in Concord *(see
p.47)*. At **Chesterwood** (4 Williamsville
Road; tel: 413-298-3579; www.chester
wood.org; May–Oct daily 10am–5pm;
charge), a mile (1.5km) to the west, you
can see his plaster casts and models in
the Barn Gallery, as well as explore the
formal gardens and woodland paths
designed by French himself.

Lenox

Eight miles (13km) north of Stock-
bridge on Route 7A is the quintessential
Berkshires village of **Lenox ❸**, home to
the summer **Tanglewood Music Fes-
tival** *(see p.23)* and the **Haven Café and
Bakery**, see ⑪②. Celebrated author
Edith Wharton (1862–1937) built her
Georgian Revival summer residence
The Mount (2 Plunkett Street; tel:
413-551-5111; www.edithwharton.org;
May–Oct daily 10am–5pm; charge) in
Lenox in 1902. Three acres (1.2ha) of
lush formal gardens have been recreated
to Wharton's original design.

Shaker Village

Drive north to **Pittsfield** and then
west for 4 miles (6.5km) on Route 20 to
the **Hancock Shaker Village ❹** (tel:
413-443-0188; www.hancockshakervil
lage.org; winter 10am–3pm, summer
9.30am–5pm), an immaculately preserved reminder of the Shaker religious
movement, which peaked in the US in
the early 19th century. The buildings,
farm, and a store selling Shaker reproduction furniture and goods illustrate
the sect's devotion to orderly simplicity.

North Adams

From Pittsfield, follow Route 8 for 21
miles (34km) north to **North Adams
❺**, an old industrial town that's under-
gone something of a revival since the
creation of the exciting and enormous
**Massachusetts Museum of Con-
temporary Arts** (MASS MoCA; 87

Marshall Street; tel: 413-662-2111; www.massmoca.org; daily 10am–6pm; charge) that dominates downtown *(see margin, left)*. Stay at **The Porches Inn** *(see p.109)* and dine at the museum's **Café Latino**, see ③.

PIONEER VALLEY

Along the scenic 30-mile (48km) drive east to Greenfield on Route 2, pause at the picturesque village of **Shelburne Falls ❻**, where the unusual **Bridge of Flowers** (www.bridgeofflowersmass. org; free), a 1908 trolley bridge, is now a pedestrian walkway turned into a delightful garden.

Return to the Pioneer Valley at **Greenfield** and head south, following the course of the Connecticut River. After 3 miles (5km) on Route 5 is **Historic Deerfield ❼** (The Street; tel: 413-775-7133; www.historic-deerfield. org; mid-Apr–end Nov daily 9.30am– 4.30pm; charge), a beautifully preserved village commemorating the life of New England pioneers in 11 museum homes. There are guided walks and demonstrations of traditional pioneer ways of life. The **Deerfield Inn** *(see pp.108–9)* provides excellent food and lodging.

Amherst and Northampton
It's a 15-mile (24km) drive south to the collegiate town of **Amherst ❽** on Route 5 then 116. The **Emily Dickinson Homestead** (280 Main Street; tel: 413-542-8161; guided tours only) preserves

the belongings of the poet who lived in the town throughout her life (1830–86). Nearby is **The Black Sheep**, see ①④.

Finish up in the nearby town of **Northampton ❾**, home of **Smith College** (www.smith.edu), a liberal arts institution for women. This attractive place, described by Swedish opera singer Jenny Lind in 1850 as the 'Paradise of America,' has a great selection of places to eat, including **Lhasa Café**, see ①⑤.

From Northampton back to Springfield it is 22 miles (35km) down I-91.

Deerfield Raids
In 1704 raiders from French Canada and their Indian allies descended on Deerfield, where they massacred many of the inhabitants and carried more than 100 off to captivity in Quebec.

Food and Drink

② HAVEN CAFÉ AND BAKERY
8 Franklin Street, Lenox; tel: 413-637-8948; Mon–Wed and Sat 8am–3pm, Thur–Fri until 8pm, Sun until 2pm; $–$$
A stylish self-serve operation, with a tempting range of baked goods, breakfast dishes, and meals made with local produce.

③ CAFÉ LATINO
1111 MASS MoCA Way, North Adams; tel: 413-662-2004; www.cafelatinoatmoca.com; Thur–Sat 11.30am–3pm, 5–9pm, Sun 11.30am–3pm; $$
Enjoy modern Mexican-style cooking, such as quesadilla with homemade chorizo, at this stylish restaurant bar.

④ THE BLACK SHEEP
79 Main Street, Amherst; tel: 413-253-3442; www.black sheepdeli.com; Mon–Thur 7am–8pm, Fri–Sat 7am–9pm, Sun 7.30am–8pm; $
Hang with the students at this appealingly rustic deli, with creative sandwiches, great drinks, and irresistible baked goods.

⑤ LHASA CAFÉ
159 Main Street, Northampton; tel: 413-586-5427; www.lhasacafe.com; Mon–Thur noon–3pm, 5–9.30pm, Fri–Sat noon–10pm, Sun noon–9.30pm; $–$$
The authentic Tibetan cooking here includes freshly made *mo-mo* (dumplings) and yak-meat dishes. They offer a good lunch deal Monday to Friday.

PROVIDENCE

A walk around Rhode Island's handsome capital, which has outstanding 18th- and 19th-century architecture, an excitingly rejuvenated downtown, and a vibrant, arty scene thanks to its prestigious universities and colleges.

Tourist Information
Providence's Visitor Information Service (1 Sabin Street; tel: 401-751-1177; www. goprovidence.com; Mon–Sat 9am–5pm) is at the Rhode Island Convention Center.

DISTANCE 4 miles (6.5km)
TIME A full day
START State House
END Prospect Terrace
POINTS TO NOTE

Providence is an easy day trip from Boston (51 miles/82km southwest); there is parking beside the Amtrak station. Newport is 38 miles (61km) farther south (see p.66).

STATE HOUSE

The white marble dome of **Rhode Island State House** ❶ (Smith Street; tel: 401-222-3983; www.rilin.state. ri.us; reserve ahead for tours Mon–Fri at 9, 10, 11am, noon, and 1pm; free) dominates Constitution Hill. Inside, you will find the 1663 charter in which Charles II created the Colony of Rhode Island and Providence Plantations – still the state's official name.

Head south down Francis Street past Providence Place Mall; to the left is **Waterplace Park ❷**, an Italian-inspired piazza beside the river; come here from April to October to enjoy the night-time **WaterFire** (www.waterfire. org) displays; see the website for dates.

Walking Tours
Recommended 90-minute walking tours of the Benefit Street area depart from the John Brown House Museum Tue–Sat at 11am mid-June–mid-Oct (see www.rihs.org for details).

DOWNTOWN

Cross the river and proceed to **Kennedy Plaza**, from where buses to Boston and Newport depart. Nearby are many grand edifices, including the Art Deco **Industrial Trust Building ❸**, now housing a branch of Bank of America; the **Turk's Head Building ❹** (1 Turk's Head Place), a 1913 landmark with an ornate stone head over its entrance; and the handsome Greek Revival **Arcade** (1828; 65 Weybosset Street), the nation's first indoor shopping mall (currently closed).

One side of the Arcade is on **Westminster Street**, which exemplifies Downtown's revival with trendy boutiques and eateries, including **Tazza**, see ⑪①, and the cheeseshop and deli **Farmstead** (no. 123; www.farmstead inc.com; Mon–Fri 11am–7pm, Sat noon–6pm). Around the corner on Washington Street more tasty food can be found at **Local 121**, see ⑪②.

BENEFIT STREET

Walk back along Westminster Street and cross the river to explore **Benefit Street ❺**, along and around which are

more than 200 restored 18th- and
19th-century buildings. The Providence
Preservation Society (http://ppsri.org)
rescued the area from the neglected state
it was in barely 30 years ago.

John Brown House Museum

Continue south along Benefit Street
and turn left into Power Street to reach
the home described by John Quincy
Adams as 'the most magnificent and
elegant private mansion that I have ever
seen on this continent.' Judge for yourself on a tour around the **John Brown
House Museum** ❻ (no. 52; tel: 401-
273-7507; www.rihs.org; tours Tue–Fri
1 and 3pm, Sat 10.30am, noon, 1.30 and
3pm; charge), packed with period
furniture, paintings, porcelain, and
mementoes of the 'Old China Trade.'

Brown University and RISD

Turn left onto Brown Street and proceed towards the campus of **Brown
University** ❼ (College Hill; http://
brown.edu). Founded in 1764, this Ivy
League institution moved to Providence
in 1770. To the east is the student,
commercial strip of Thayer Street.

Return to Benefit Street to explore the
fantastic **Rhode Island School of
Design Museum** ❽ (no. 224; tel: 401-
454-6500; www.risdmuseum.org; Sept–
July Tue–Sun 10am–5pm; charge).
Among its collection of over 84,000 art-
works are fragments from Pompeii,
Yemeni tribal dresses and paintings by
Picasso, Monet, and Damien Hirst.

Prospect Terrace

Pass behind the **First Baptist Church
in America** (www.fbcia.org; Mon–Fri
10am–noon, 1–3pm, Sat 10am–1pm;
charge), established in 1638, and continue to South Court Street. Climb
the hill to **Prospect Terrace** ❾ park
(Congdon Street), presided over by a
statue of Roger Williams, Providence's
founder, who is buried here.

Food and Drink

① TAZZA

250 Westminster Street; tel: 401-421-3300; http://tazzacaffe.
com; Mon 7am–10pm, Tue and Wed 7am–midnight, Thur
7am–1am, Fri 7am–2am, Sat 8am–2am, Sun 8am–5pm; $
A hipster café-bar that buzzes from breakfast until late.

② LOCAL 121

121 Washington Street; tel: 401-274-2121; www.local121.
com; Mon 5–10pm, Tue–Thur noon–3pm and 5–10pm, Fri
noon–3pm and 5–11pm, Sat 5–11pm, Sun 5–9pm; $$$
Dishes incorporating top-grade New England ingredients
are served at this elegant restaurant.

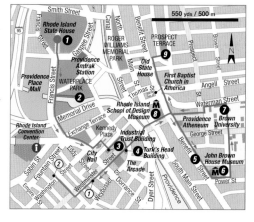

8

NEWPORT

Stacked with gilded Great Gatsby-esque mansions that their 19th-century millionaire owners referred to as 'summer cottages,' Newport commands a stunning position on Rhode Island's coast.

Cliff Walk
Examine the back-yards of the mansions from the Cliff Walk (http://cliffwalk.com), a 3½-mile (5.5km) path hugging the Rhode Island Sound.

DISTANCE 3 miles (5km)

TIME A full day

START Gateway Visitor Center

END Marble House

POINTS TO NOTE

This tour can be combined with that of Providence *(see p.64)* and a frequent Ripta bus service (1 hour; www.ripta.com) links the two. If driving, park at the Gateway Visitor Center where you will also find Newport's Visitor Information Center (23 America's Cup Avenue; tel: 800-976-5122; http://go newport.com; daily 9am–5pm).

Food and Drink 🍽️

① BLACK PEARL
Bannister's Wharf; tel: 401-846-5264; www.blackpearl newport.com; daily noon–1am; $$
Popular among the yachting set, this harborside place is very reliable and offers a range of dishes from seafood snacks and sandwiches to grilled meats and fish.

② THE WHITE HORSE TAVERN
26 Marlborough Street; tel: 401-849-3600; www.white horsetavern.us; daily 11.30am–10pm; $$$
The country's oldest operating tavern (1673) serves fine-dining American cuisine, with dishes such as Vermont goat's cheese-cake, New England lobster sauté, and Georges Bank flounder.

DOWNTOWN

Begin at the **Gateway Visitor Center** *(see left)*, then walk south along America's Cup Avenue to the **Museum of Newport History ❶** (127 Thames Street; tel: 401-846-0813; http://new porthistorical.org; Tue–Sun 10am–5pm; donation), on the left in the restored 1762 Brick Market building.

Follow Touro Street to no. 85 to find the **Touro Synagogue ❷** (tel: 401-847-4794; www.tourosynagogue.org; tours Sun–Fri except Jewish holidays; charge). Built in 1763, it is the nation's oldest Jewish house of worship.

Walk south down Spring Street to Queen Anne Square, home to the white clapboard 1725–6 **Trinity Episcopal Church ❸** (tel: 401-846-0660; www.trinitynewport.org), said to be based on the designs of Sir Christopher Wren. Walk a block west to Newport Harbor to lunch at the **Black Pearl**, see 🍽️①.

BELLEVUE AVENUE

Many of Newport's attractions line the thoroughfare of **Bellevue Avenue**, a few blocks to the east. The 1862 **Newport Art Museum ❹** (no. 76; tel: 401-848-

8200; www.newportartmuseum.org; Tue–Sat 10am–5pm, Sun noon–5pm; charge) exhibits works by George Innes, Winslow Homer, and regional artists.

Housed in the Newport Casino is the **International Tennis Hall of Fame** ❺ (no. 194; tel: 401-849-3990; www.tennisfame.com; daily 9.30am–5pm; charge). Despite the building's name, it never had anything to do with gambling, but was America's most exclusive country club when it opened in 1880 and hosted the first US National Tennis Championships the following year.

THE MANSIONS

If you plan to tour several mansions, the **Preservation Society of Newport** ❻ (242 Bellevue Avenue; tel: 401-847-1000; http://newportmansions.org) sells various tickets for admission to up to 11 properties and offers tours; check their website, as seasons and hours at the properties vary greatly. The following are recommended, if time is limited.

Coal-rich Edward Julius Berwind commissioned **The Elms** ❼ (367 Bellevue Avenue; charge), based on Château d'Asnières near Paris. It borrows from a range of styles, including Chinese, Venetian, and Louis XIV, and is surrounded by gorgeous gardens. Sign up for the 'behind the scenes' tour to see the mansion from the servants' point of view as well as to go up on the roof.

An opulent Italian Renaissance palace, completed in 1895 for Cornelius Vanderbilt II, **The Breakers** ❽ (44 Ochre Point; charge) is considered the most magnificent of the Newport cottages, with rooms extravagantly adorned with marble, alabaster, gilt, mosaic, crystal, and stained glass. The kitchen alone is the size of a small house.

Built in 1892 for William K. Vanderbilt and styled after the Grand and Petit Trianons of Versailles, **Marble House** ❾ (596 Bellevue Avenue; charge) upstages The Breakers for ostentation, although it is not as large. A Chinese tea-house stands in the grounds.

End your day with a meal at the **White Horse Tavern**, see ⑪②.

Above from far left: The Breakers in winter; Trinity Episcopal Church.

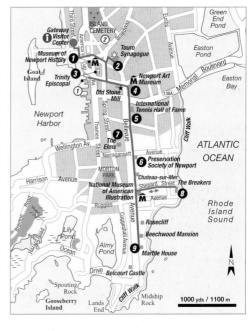

CONNECTICUT COAST

Visit pirate islands, ride a steam train, and sail a riverboat down the Connecticut River on this road trip shadowing the Long Island Sound from venerable Yale University to the old port of Mystic.

DISTANCE 86½ miles (139km)

TIME Two days

START New Haven

END Mystic

POINTS TO NOTE

Note that Yale's museums are closed on Monday. From Mystic, hop onto I-95 for 50 miles (81km) to reach Providence *(see p.64)* or turn off after 19 miles (31km) onto Route 138 for Newport *(see p.66)*. It is 86 miles (138km) via Hartford to Springfield *(see p.60)*. New Haven and Mystic are also connected with Boston by Amtrak's Northeast Regional line.

New Haven Details

For general tourist information, head to the Greater New Haven Convention and Visitor Bureau (169 Orange Street; tel: 203-777-8550; www.visitnewhaven. com; Mon–Fri 8.30am–5pm).

This drive from New Haven, home of Ivy League university Yale, to the old whaling port turned tourist town of Mystic, reveals the multifaceted layers of Connecticut's coast, where historic villages of traditional inns and antiques shops lie alongside the working naval towns of New London and Groton.

NEW HAVEN AND YALE UNIVERSITY

Settled by Puritans in 1638, **New Haven ❶** was at first a seafaring community, but later embraced industry and pioneered such inventions as the meat grinder, the corkscrew, and the steamboat. Today, it is known as the home of

Food and Drink

① **LOUIS' LUNCH**

261–263 Crown Street, New Haven; tel: 203-562-5507; www. louislunch.com; Tue–Wed 11am–4pm, Thur–Sat noon–2am; $

Devour flame-grilled patties on white toast and strictly no ketchup at this Yale institution.

② **SCOOZZI TRATTORIA**

1104 Chapel Street, New Haven; tel: 203-776-8268; www.scoozzi.com; Tue–Fri noon–2.30pm, 5–9pm, Sat noon–9.30pm, Sun noon–3pm, 5–8.30pm; $$$

A modern Italian restaurant with a great reputation and a pleasant outdoor patio area, close to the Yale landmarks.

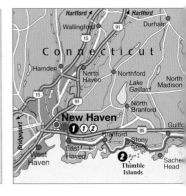

prestigious **Yale University**. Founded in 1701 and named after its benefactor, Elihu Yale, the US's third-oldest university is *alma mater* to many presidents, including Bill Clinton and both Bushes.

Park close to **New Haven Green**, the town's center, and walk to the **Yale University Visitor Center** (149 Elm Street; tel: 203-432-2300; http://yale.edu; Mon–Fri 9am–4.30pm, Sat–Sun 11am–4pm; free) on the green's north side. Pick up a map or join one of the 95-minute **campus tours** (Mon–Fri 10.30am and 2pm, Sat–Sun 1.30pm).

A classic example of the Ivy League Gothic Revival style of the early 20th century, the campus's attractions include the **University Art Gallery** (111 Chapel Street; tel: 203-432-0600; Tue–Sat 10am–5pm, Sun 1–6pm; free), with a rich collection of early American decorative and contemporary fine art, and the excellent **Yale Center for British Art** (1080 Chapel Street; tel: 203-432-2800; Tue–Sat 10am–5pm, Sun noon–

5pm; free), which boasts the largest collection of British art outside the UK, with works by Turner and Constable.

Take a break at either **Louis' Lunch**, see ⑪①, or **Scoozzi Trattoria**, see ⑪②.

THIMBLE ISLANDS

Head east on routes 1 and 146 for 14 miles (22.5km) to the tiny seaside village of **Stony Creek**, embarkation point for a 45-minute boat trip to the **Thimble Islands ②** (tel: 203-488-8905; www.thimbleislandcruise.com; May and Sept Fri–Sun, June–Aug Wed–Mon, Oct Sat–Sun, check website for times; charge), 354 rugged outcrops peppered with mansions, summer homes, and stories dating back to Captain Kidd.

HAMMONASSET BEACH

Hammonasset Beach ③, 12 miles (19km) farther along routes 146 and 1, is Connecticut's largest waterfront

Above from far left: students make their way to Yale University; Five Mile Point, New Haven Harbor; *Charles W. Morgan* at Mystic Seaport Museum.

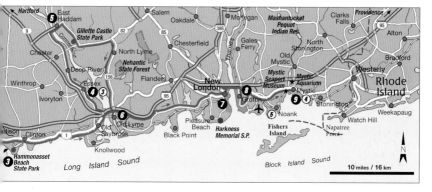

Above from left:
Connecticut River Museum; Essex Steam Train.

state park. It occupies an entire peninsula, with ample room for swimming, fishing, hiking, and camping (tel: 203-245-2785 for bookings).

ESSEX

Overlooking the Connecticut River, the genteel town of **Essex ❹**, 17 miles (10.5km) farther east (via Route 1 and, for a short way, north along Route 9) typifies upscale Yankeedom. Check out the restored 18th-century homes, a riverfront dotted with sailboats, and the rambling 1776 **Griswold Inn** *(see p.110)*. Stroll down to the wharfside **Connecticut River Museum** (67 Main Street; tel: 860-767-8269; www. ctrivermuseum.org; Tue–Sun 10am–5pm; charge), which has a working

Mystic Information
The Mystic and Shoreline Visitor Information Center (27 Coogan Boulevard; tel: 860-536-1614; www.mysticinfo.com; Mon–Sat 9am–6pm, Sun 9am–4.30pm) is next to Olde Mystick Village on the north edge of town.

model of the world's first submarine, a design of Yale student David Bushnell in 1776. Grab a bite to eat at the **Crow's Nest Restaurant**, see ⑪③.

EAST HADDAM

Ditch the car for an excursion on the **Essex Steam Train and Riverboat** (1 Railroad Avenue; tel: 860-767-0103 or 800-377-3987; www.essexsteamtrain. com; charge) to **East Haddam ❺**. The train, drawn by a 1926 locomotive, clatters north to Deep River Landing, where you change to the riverboat; the entire round trip takes about two and a half hours. If you would rather drive, follow Route 154 north then Route 82 east; it is 10 miles (16km) in all.

In East Haddam visit the **Goodspeed Opera House** (6 Main Street; tel: 860-873-8668; www.goodspeed.org), a riverside theatre dating from 1876. A 4-mile (6.5km) drive south is **Gillette Castle State Park** (67 River Road; tel: 860-526-2336; daily 8am–dusk; free), home to an imposing stone '**castle**,' (Memorial Day–Labor Day daily 10am–4.30pm; charge), built in 1914 by eccentric actor William Gillette.

Hartford

Connecticut's capital, Hartford, 37 miles (60km) inland from New Haven, may not be the most buzzing of New England cities, but it's not without attractions. The Mark Twain House (351 Farmington Avenue; tel: 860-247-0998; www. marktwainhouse.org; Mon–Sat 9.30am–5.30pm, Sun noon–5.30pm, closed Tue Jan–Mar; charge) is a quirky 1874 mansion decorated by Louis Tiffany. The Wadsworth Atheneum (600 Main Street; tel: 860-278-2670; www.wadsworth atheneum.org; Wed–Fri 11am–5pm, Sat–Sun 10am–5pm; charge) features Baroque, Impressionist, and 19th-century American works, plus a collection of 17th-century furniture. The impressive State Capitol (210 Capitol Avenue; tel: 860-240-0222; Mon–Fri 8am–5pm; free) overlooks lovely Bushnell Park. For more details, see www.enjoyhartford.com.

OLD LYME

For a more evocative view of the region's golden past, drive south from East Haddam on routes 82 and 156, which pass through the peaceful countryside that borders Connecticut's west

shore. Pause in **Old Lyme** ➏ to visit the **Florence Griswold Museum** (96 Lyme Street; tel: 860-434-5542; www. florencegriswoldmuseum.org; Tue–Sat 10am–5pm, Sun 1–5pm; charge), which has a renowned collection of American Impressionist paintings and recalls the village's heyday as an artists' colony at the start of the 20th century.

NEW LONDON AND GROTON

In the old whaling port of **New London** ➐, 15 miles (24km) east of Old Lyme at the mouth of the Thames River, you will find the **US Coast Guard Academy** (31 Mohegan Avenue; www.cga.edu; cadet-led and self-guided tours daily 9am–4.30pm; free), where the magnificent sailing vessel *Eagle* (tours when in port; tel: 860-444-8595) is used for training coast-guard cadets.

Groton ➑, on the other side of the Thames, is home to the **US Navy Submarine Force Museum** (1 Crystal Lake Road; tel: 860-694-3174; www. ussnautilus.org; Wed–Mon May–Oct 9am–5pm, Nov–Apr 9am–4pm; free), where you can peek inside the *Nautilus*, the USA's first nuclear submarine.

MYSTIC

With its picture-perfect harbour, **Mystic** ➒, 6 miles (10km) east of Groton, is one of the principal tourist draws of the state's coast.

At the mouth of the Mystic River is the **Mystic Seaport Museum** (75 Greenmanville Avenue; tel: 860-572-5315; www.mysticseaport.org; daily 9am–5pm; charge), a living history museum spread across 17 acres (7ha), where you will find early 19th-century wharves, stores, and houses. Costumed actors demonstrate crafts and cooking techniques. The collection of some 500 vessels includes the wooden whaling ship *Charles W. Morgan* and a replica of the *Amistad* slave ship.

Mystic offers dozens of dining choices; try **Mystic Pizza**, see ⑪④, the classy Italian restaurant **Bravo Bravo** (tel: 860-536-3228) beneath the **Whaler's Inn** *(see p.110)*, or drive 1¹⁄₂ miles (2.5km) to **Noank** and **Abbot's Lobster in the Rough**, see ⑪⑤.

Mystic Aquarium

Out of town near I-95, the Mystic Aquarium (55 Coogan Boulevard; tel: 860-572-5955; www.mysticaquarium.org; daily Mar–Oct 9am–5pm, Nov 9am–4pm, Dec–Feb 10am–4pm; charge) numbers seals, sea lions, and beluga whales among its collection of 12,000 fish, invertebrates, and marine mammals. It is also the home of the high-tech Institute for Exploration, with exhibits and a simulated deep-sea dive devised by Robert Ballard, who discovered the wreck of the *Titanic*.

Food and Drink 🍴

③ CROW'S NEST RESTAURANT
35 Pratt Street, Essex; tel: 860-767-3288; Sun–Wed 7am–4pm, Thur–Sat 7am–9pm; $$
This convivial café, with a good view of Essex's marina, serves sandwiches, salads, and seafood and meat dishes.

④ MYSTIC PIZZA
56 West Main Street, Mystic; tel: 860-536-3737; www.mysticpizza.com; daily 10am–10.30pm; $–$$
A homely pizza joint that inspired the eponymous 1988 movie starring Julia Roberts.

⑤ ABBOT'S LOBSTER IN THE ROUGH
117 Pearl Street, Noank; tel: 860-536-7719; www.abbotslobster.com; mid-May–early Sept daily noon–9pm, Sept–mid-May Fri–Sun noon–7pm; $$
Head to the waterfront to enjoy fresh lobster and other seafood dishes alfresco with bring-your-own drinks.

THE GREEN MOUNTAINS

This two-day drive along the VT 100, the meandering backbone of Vermont, takes you straight to the leafy heart of this laid-back state and ends at the sophisticated town of Woodstock, close to the premier ski resort of Killington.

Countryside Walks
A great way to discover Vermont's countryside is to follow the self-guided walking routes organized by Vermont Inn-to-Inn Walking Tours (tel: 1-800-822-8799; www.vermontinntoinnwalking.com) around the towns of Chester and Ludlow, the latter on Route 100, 10 miles (16km) north of Weston.

DISTANCE 83 miles (134km)

TIME Two days

START Brattleboro

END Woodstock

POINTS TO NOTE

This route can connect with the Berkshires to the south *(see p.60).* You can join the Lake Champlain Valley tour *(see p.76)* by driving 46 miles (74km) north from Woodstock to Brandon along Route 7. Or head east for 70 miles (113km) via Route 4 to Meredith in the Lakes Region of New Hampshire *(see p.80).*

Nearly every image conjured by the name 'Vermont' comes to life along this leisurely itinerary, ticking off the picturesque little villages and arty towns that line the southern half of scenic Route 100. You will see rolling dairy farms dotted with black-and-white cows and the tree-covered slopes of the Green Mountains. The spectacular fall colors are world-famous.

BRATTLEBORO

With a granola-and-sandals bohemian atmosphere, **Brattleboro ❶**, on the banks of the Connecticut River, will provide a relaxed start to your trip. Near the site of Vermont's first permanent settlement and founded in 1724, Brattleboro had been a busy manufacturing center in the 19th century, but was on the downturn by the 20th century. Concerned local artists and activists came to the rescue, founding the Brattleboro Arts Initiative (www.brattleboroarts.org) in 1998.

Among the initiative's successes has been its taking over of the stylish Art Deco **Latchis Memorial Building** (50 Main Street), which includes a hotel *(see p.110)* and adjacent cinema, the

Food and Drink 🍴

① FLAT STREET BREW PUB AND TAP ROOM
6 Flat Street, Brattleboro; tel: 802-257-1911; www.flatstreetbrewpub.net; daily pub 4–11pm, restaurant 5–9.30pm; $$
Upstairs in the pub and downstairs in the restaurant you can enjoy a great range of locally brewed ales along with hearty meals, including chunky burgers and big salads.

② CURTIS' ALL AMERICAN BAR-BE-CUE PIT
7 Putney Landing Road, Putney; tel: 802-387-5474; www.curtisbbqvt.com; Wed–Sun 10am–dusk; $
Curtis' barbecued pork ribs and chicken with sides are delicious, even though the food comes out of two school buses turned into kitchens.

latter a nostalgic gem that harks back to the glamorous days of movie-going. Also within the building is the lively **Flat Street Brew Pub and Tap Room**, see ⑪①.

Across the way, at 10 Vernon Street, the **Brattleboro Museum and Art Center** (tel: 802-257-0124; www.brattleboromuseum.org; Wed–Mon 11am–5pm; charge) recounts local history, and hosts changing art exhibitions as well as occasional music events.

Head 7 miles (11km) north to Putney, via I-91, for a fine feed at **Curtis' All American Bar-be-cue Pit**, see ⑪②.

NEWFANE TO WESTON

For the 50-mile (80km) drive to Weston, first follow Route 30 along the West River valley, heading north at Rawsonville onto Route 100. En route you will pass through a series of pretty Vermont settlements centered on village greens. **Newfane ❷** (www.newfanevt.com) is one of the most attractive, with its 1825 Greek Revival county courthouse, whitewashed churches, and cluster of antiques shops. The town hosts a **flea market** May to October every Sunday from 6am on Route 30.

Scott Bridge

About 6 miles (10km) north of Newfane, pause to inspect the **Scott Bridge ❸**. Built in 1870, and now open only to pedestrians, the 275ft (85m) covered structure is Vermont's longest

wooden bridge. You will spot several such covered bridges along this route and elsewhere in New England; their design helps protect the bridges' frames from the elements.

Stratton Mountain

Routes 30 and 100 join at East Jamaica, continuing together for 8 miles (13km) along the east boundary of the **Green Mountain National Forest** (www.fs.fed.us/r9/forests/greenmountain).

You are now entering the heart of south Vermont's ski country, with the slopes of **Stratton Mountain** looming to the left. For panoramic vistas during foliage season, go west for 4 miles (6.5km) on Route 30 from Rawsonville

Fall Colors
It depends on the weather, but the peak of the fall foliage season falls typically between mid-October and early November.

to ride the **Stratton Gondola ❹** (Route 1; tel: 802-297-2200; www.stratton. com; July–late Sept Sat–Sun 10am–5pm, foliage season late Sept–mid-Oct daily; charge) to the peak. Otherwise, keep heading north along Route 100. A short way along is the pretty village of **South Londonderry**, home of **Village Pantry De Logis**, see ⓉⓅ③.

WESTON

The next stop along Route 100 is pristine **Weston ❺**, where the ample town green is circled by homes dating back to the 1790s. On the green, the **Weston Playhouse** (tel: 802-824-5288; www. westonplayhouse.org; late June–early Sept) has hosted summer theater productions for over 60 years and has a polished reputation.

Vermont Country Store

Most visitors are drawn to Weston by the celebrated **Vermont Country Store** (657 Main Street; tel: 802-824-3184; www.vermontcountrystore.com; daily 9am–5.30pm), a throwback to the small-town emporia of a century ago. With a potbellied stove and a penny-candy counter, the store has grown into an omnium-gatherum of all sorts of practical items. When it comes to lunch, the store's **Bryant House**, see ⓉⓅ④, is a good bet. If you are staying the night, **The Inn at Weston** *(see p.110)* has comfortable rooms and fine dining.

PLYMOUTH NOTCH HISTORIC DISTRICT

Calvin Coolidge was one of two US presidents born in Vermont (the other was Chester A. Arthur). Coolidge's ancestral village of **Plymouth Notch ❻**, located in the hills 32 miles (51km) north of Weston via routes 100 and 100A, is preserved as the **Plymouth Notch Historic District** (tel: 802-672-3773; www.historicvermont.org; late May–mid-Oct daily 9.30am–5pm; charge). You can see Coolidge's father's general store, the family's cheese company, and the house in which he took the oath of office on August 2, 1923, when, as vice-president, he learned of President Harding's death. A dyed-in-the-wool conservative Yankee, Coolidge would no doubt approve if he could see how little Plymouth Notch has changed.

Killington

Some of New England's best skiing is to be found at Killington (tel: 802-422-3261/1-800-621-6867; www.killing ton.com), 20 miles (32km) west of Woodstock. Offering 200 runs over seven mountains and a drop of over 3,000ft (900m), this is Vermont's premier ski resort, with a season that runs from late November to late May. When the snow melts, it becomes a destination for mountain bikers, who coast down some 45 miles (72km) of trails. For accommodation options, check the resort's website.

WOODSTOCK

It is another Vermont altogether at **Woodstock ❼**, 17 miles (27km) east of Plymouth Notch via routes 100A and 4. The roaring Ottauquechee River here once powered wool mills, and it was on a nearby hillside in 1934 that the state's first ski tow presaged Vermont's modern tourist economy. Also instrumental in Woodstock's transformation was the late Laurance Rockefeller's acquisition of the **Woodstock Inn** *(see p.111)*, which he turned into one of Vermont's plushest hostelries.

Woodstock's town center, a sophisticated place of galleries, boutiques, and cafés, is surrounded by block after block of handsomely restored Federal and Greek Revival homes. For lunch, try **Alléchante**, see ⑪⑤, or head 7 miles (11km) out of town to **The Farmers Diner**, see ⑪⑥, in **Quechee**.

Marsh-Billings-Rockefeller National Historical Park

Well worth exploring are the mansion and grounds at **Marsh-Billings-Rockefeller National Historical Park** (tel: 802-457-3368; www.nps.gov/mabi; late May–Oct daily 10am–5pm; grounds free, mansion charge), just out of town on Route 12. This 500-acre (200ha) woodland tract, threaded with hiking trails and carriage roads, honors George Perkins Marsh, a 19th-century Woodstock native and early conservationist, who advised the property's owner, the railroad magnate and gentleman farmer Frederick Billings.

On the other side of Route 12 is the **Billings Farm and Museum** (tel: 802-457-2355; www.billingsfarm.org; May–late Oct daily 10am–5pm, Nov–Feb Sat–Sun 10am–3.30pm; charge), a working model farm since Billings's day. In addition to its prize dairy herd, the farm features an excellent collection of antique farm implements and local-history exhibits. Guided tours and demonstrations allow you to experience farm work at first hand.

Food and Drink

③ VILLAGE PANTRY DE LOGIS
1 Main Street, South Londonderry; tel: 802-824-9800; www.villagepantry.com; daily 7am–7pm; $
Drop by this provider of high-quality gourmet takeaways and coffee for the road.

④ BRYANT HOUSE
Route 100, Weston; tel: 802-824-6287; daily 11.30am–3.30pm, Fri–Sat 3.30–8pm; $$
The old-fashioned home-style cooking served here includes chicken pie with gravy and pancakes that come with a souvenir bottle of local maple syrup.

⑤ ALLÉCHANTE
61 Central Street, Woodstock; tel: 802-457-3300; www.allechantevt.com; daily 8am–5pm; $–$$
This cute café dishes up homemade savory tarts, pastries, and wonderfully prepared foods, all using local ingredients.

⑥ THE FARMERS DINER
5573 Woodstock Road, Quechee Gorge Village, Quechee; tel: 802-295-4600; www.farmersdiner.com; Tue–Wed 7am–3pm, Thur–Mon 7am–8pm; $
Enjoy delicious comfort food, with ingredients sourced from local farmers, in this diner set in a wood-paneled dining car.

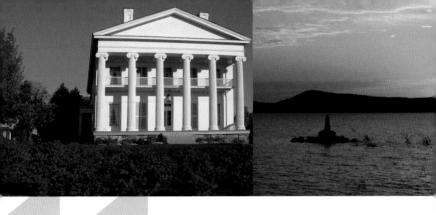

BURLINGTON AND LAKE CHAMPLAIN VALLEY

On the east shore of beautiful Lake Champlain is Burlington, Vermont's largest and most diverse city. From here, this driving tour rambles through the broad Champlain valley and lofty passes of the Green Mountains.

Above from left: stately Burlington architecture; Lake Champlain; the *Ticonderoga* at the Shelburne Museum.

DISTANCE 130 miles (209km) round trip
TIME Two days
START/END Burlington
POINTS TO NOTE

If you are connecting from the Green Mountains route *(see p.72)*, begin at Brandon. Amtrak's Vermonter train stops in Essex Junction, 5 miles (8km) east of Burlington, and Burlington International Airport (www.burlingtonintl airport.com) is 3 miles (5km) east. Meredith, in the Lakes Region of New Hampshire *(see p.80)*, is 147 miles (237km) southeast via I-89 and Route 4.

BURLINGTON

Island Line Trail
Rent a bike from Local Motion in Burlington (1 Steele Street; tel: 802-652-2453; www.local motion.org) to cycle the 12-mile (19km) Island Line Trail that skirts the edge of Lake Champlain.

Vermont's 'Queen City,' **Burlington ❶** enjoys a hillside location facing the broadest part of Lake Champlain. Orientate yourself at the **Waterfront Park** and adjacent **ECHO Lake Aquarium & Science Center** (1 College Street; tel: 877-324-6386; www.echovermont.org; daily 10am–

5pm; charge). Here, exhibits explain the natural history of the 125-mile (200km) long lake and explore the mystery of Champ, its mythical aquatic monster. Nearby, grab a crêpe at **Skinny Pancake**, see ⑪①.

Ferries and Boats

From the King Street landing, just south of the park, car and passenger **ferries** (tel: 802-864-9804; www.fer ries.com) make the one-hour crossing to Port Kent, New York. Alternatively, take a trip on the cruise ship *Spirit of Ethan Allen II* (Burlington Community Boathouse; tel: 802-862-8300; www.soea.com) or the *Friend Ship* **sloop** (tel: 802-598-6504; www.whist lingman.com), or rent a kayak or canoe from **Waterfront Boat Rentals** (Perkins Pier; tel: 802-864-4858; www. waterfrontboatrentals.com).

Downtown

Burlington's lively downtown is dominated by pedestrianised Church Street, with its bistros, boutiques, and craft galleries such as the **Vermont Craft Center Frog Hollow** (no. 85;

www.froghollow.org), exhibiting works by Vermont artisans. For a meal, stop in at **Penny Cluse Café**, see ⑪②, or **Leunig's** *(see p.118)*.

University of Vermont Campus
The hilltop **University of Vermont** (UVM; www.uvm.edu) campus is worth exploring. Along University Place stand an array of college buildings, including the 1825 **Old Mill** (the cornerstone was laid by the Marquis de Lafayette), and architect H.H. Richardson's Romanesque, 1886 **Billings Student Center**.

Around the corner is the **Fleming Museum** (61 Colchester Avenue; tel: 802-656-0750; www.uvm.edu/~fleming; check website for hours; charge), with an excellent collection of European and American art, plus ethnographic exhibits from around the world.

SHELBURNE

Head south out of Burlington on Route 7 for 10 miles (16km) to **Shelburne ❶**, where the **Shelburne Museum** (tel: 802-985-3346; www.shelburnemuseum.org; May–mid-Oct daily 10am–5pm; charge) comprises one of the nation's premier collections of Americana. Largely the legacy of heiress Electra Havemeyer Webb, the vast holdings include folk art, toys, tools, and horse-drawn vehicles, arrayed among 39 buildings on 45 landscaped acres (18ha). Don't miss the *Ticonderoga*, a 1906 Lake Champlain passenger steamer.

Food and Drink

① SKINNY PANCAKE

60 Lake Street, Burlington; tel: 802-540-0188; www.skinnypancake.com; Mon 8am–2.30pm, Tue–Sun 8am–9pm; $
Fill up on all kinds of crêpes, sweet and savory, with a view of Lake Champlain. In the evenings there is live music and fondue.

② PENNY CLUSE CAFÉ

169 Cherry Street, Burlington; tel: 802-651-8834; www.pennycluse.com; Mon–Fri 6.45am–3pm, Sat–Sun 8am–3pm; $
The gingerbread pancakes at this super-popular café (expect to wait in line) are just the yummy tip of a hearty menu of gut-busting breakfasts and lunch dishes.

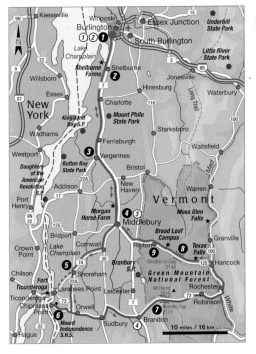

Morgan Horse Farm

To see some handsome examples of the state's official animal, the Morgan horse, head to the University of Vermont's Morgan Horse Farm (74 Battell Drive, Weybridge; tel: 802-388-2011; www.uvm.edu/morgan; May–Oct daily 9am–4pm; charge), 2 miles (3km) northwest from Middlebury. You can observe the sturdy, beautifully proportioned Morgans in their stalls, watch them graze in rolling pastures, and learn how the breed originated and acquired its status.

Shelburne Farms

Set aside a good half-day to explore **Shelburne Farms** (1611 Harbor Road; tel: 802-985-8686; www.shelburnefarms.org; mid-May–mid-Oct 10am–5pm, grounds open year-round; charge), the Webbs' country estate and model farm. You can view cheese-making and other enterprises as well as explore the beautiful lakeside grounds. Children will love encountering the various farmyard animals. The 1880s Farm and Breeding Barns are magnificent, and you can stay at Dr William Seward and Lila Vanderbilt Webb's grand home, now the **Inn at Shelburne Farms** *(see p.111)*.

VERGENNES

The small town of **Vergennes ❸**, 14 miles (23km) south of Shelburne, has delightful Victorian architecture as well as the **Lake Champlain Maritime Museum** (4472 Basin Harbor Road; tel: 802-475-2022; www.lcmm.org; May–mid-Oct daily 10am–5pm; charge). The exhibits, including a collection of antique watercraft and a replica of the *Philadelphia*, a Revolutionary War gunboat, relate the history of navigation on the lake. Down the road a good place to stay is the **Basin Harbor Club** resort *(see p.111)*.

MIDDLEBURY

Straddling the gushing waters of Otter's Creek is the attractive college town of **Middlebury ❹**, 13 miles (21km) farther south via Route 7. On its west edge, the campus of Middlebury College, a 200-year-old liberal arts institution, features an interesting **Museum of Art** (Route 30; tel: 802-443-5007; http://museum.middlebury.edu; Tue–Fri 10am–5pm, Sat–Sun noon–5pm, closed Aug and most Dec; free), with Asian and Western works from antiquity to the present.

Just off the town green is the white-washed 1809 **Congregational Church**, its steeple rising 135ft (40m) in four tiers. Also downtown, in an 1829 quarry magnate's house, is the **Henry Sheldon Museum of Vermont History** (1 Park Street; tel: 802-388-2117; www.henrysheldonmuseum.org; Tue–Sat 10am–5pm; charge), with a collection of late 18th- and 19th-century Vermontiana.

For something to eat, try **Tully & Marie's**, see ⑪❸, or **The Middlebury Inn** *(see p.111)*, where you can also stay.

Food and Drink

③ TULLY & MARIE'S
7 Bakery Lane, Middlebury; tel: 802-388-4182; www.tullyandmaries.com; daily 11.30am–9pm; $$
This casual dining place has a globetrotting menu, colorful decor, and an outdoor deck overlooking Otter's Creek.

④ CAFÉ PROVENCE
11 Center Street, Brandon; tel: 802-247-9997; www.cafeprovencevt.com; Mon–Fri 11.30am–9pm, Sat–Sun 9am–9.30pm; $$–$$$
French chef Robert has locals lapping up his American diner classics, using locally grown, seasonally available produce.

Above from far left: a Vermont round barn at the Shelburne Museum; kayaking on Lake Champlain; at the wheel at the Maritime Museum in Vergennes.

CHIPMAN'S POINT

Traveling through some of Vermont's lushest dairy lands, head southwest via routes 30 and 74 for 13 miles (21km) to **Shoreham ❺**, famous for its apple crop and fresh-pressed cider. Continue south along Route 22A to **Orwell**, turn right and head west to **Chipman's Point** and **Mount Independence State Historic Site ❻** (tel: 802-948-2000; www. historicvermont.org; grounds daily, Visitor Center late May–mid-Oct daily 9.30am–5pm; charge). This historic attraction concentrates on an American fort that commanded the lake in the battle against the British during the War of Independence. Various exhibits at the Visitor Center relate the story, and marked trails point out the remaining earthworks.

GREEN MOUNTAIN NATIONAL FOREST

Retrace your route back to Orwell and continue on Route 73 through to **Brandon**. The entire core of the town (more than 200 buildings) is listed on the National Register of Historic Places. Dine at **Café Provence**, see ⑪④.

From Brandon, Route 73 climbs into the heart of the north portion of the **Green Mountain National Forest** *(see also p.73)*. The highest point, at 2,170ft (661m), along the winding 17-mile (27km) road to Route 100 is at **Brandon Gap ❼**. The **Long Trail** (www.green mountainclub.org), Vermont's 'Footpath through the Wilderness,' crosses the road here and affords hiking access to the 3,216ft (980m) summit of **Mount Horrid**.

Middlebury Gap

Follow Route 100 north for 5 miles (8km) north to **Hancock**, then turn left for the 21-mile (34km) drive toward Middlebury on Route 125. Heading west, follow a steep route through rugged terrain that peaks at the 2,144ft (653m) **Middlebury Gap ❽**. Halfway between Hancock and the gap is a right-hand turnoff for **Texas Falls**, a beautiful cascade on the Hancock branch of the White River.

Ripton

Continuing across the gap, Route 125 descends into **Ripton ❾**, the one-time summer home of Robert Frost *(see also p.84)*, where you will find the **Chipman Inn** *(see p.111)*. A couple of miles before arriving in this hamlet, you will pass through the idyllic **Bread Loaf Campus** of Middlebury College, an unmissable collection of mustard-yellow-painted buildings with emerald-green trims. Also nearby is the **Robert Frost Wayside Area**, good for picnics; across the way, a mile (1.5km) long trail through the forest is lined with quotes from the poet's works.

After Ripton, Route 125 joins with Route 7 to bring you back to Middlebury and on to Burlington.

Fort Ticonderoga
If you are interested in Revolutionary history, make the short ferry trip (tel: 802-897-7999; www.middle bury.net/tiferry; May–Oct daily) from Larrabees Point to Ticonderoga, New York, site of historic Fort Ticonderoga (tel: 518-585-2821; www. fortticonderoga.org; late May–mid-Oct daily 9.30am–5pm; charge), a bastion captured from the British in 1775 by Vermont icon Ethan Allen.

THE LAKES REGION

Shimmering at New Hampshire's heart is Lake Winnipesaukee. Dotted with over 300 islands and surrounded by forested hills, it is home to long-established vacation towns, including Wolfeboro and Weirs Beach. There are also quieter villages and smaller lakes to be enjoyed on this circular route.

DISTANCE 74 miles (119km)
TIME One to two days
START/END Wolfeboro
POINTS TO NOTE
Conway *(see p.82)* is 36 miles (58km) north; Portsmouth *(see p.86)* is 48 miles (77km) southeast.

LAKE WINNIPESAUKEE

Squashed between Lake Wentworth and **Lake Winnipesaukee**, the state's largest body of water, is **Wolfeboro ❶**.

John Wentworth, a New Hampshire governor, built a summer retreat here in 1769 – hence Wolfeboro's claim to be 'America's oldest summer resort.' A good hotel is **The Wolfeboro Inn** *(see p.111)*, and a pleasant place for a meal is **Garwoods**, see ⓘⓞ.

Drop by the quirky **Libby Museum** (tel: 603-569-1035; www.wolfeboro nh.us; June–mid-Sept Tue–Sat 10am–4pm, Sun noon–4pm; charge), on Route 109 at the far north end of town, which displays the natural history and ethnographic collection of local dentist Dr Henry Forrest Libby.

Weirs Beach
Follow Route 28 south for 10 miles (16km) to the tiny town of **Alton Bay**, then head north along Route 11 to family-friendly **Weirs Beach ❷**. Stacked with game arcades such as the enormous **Funspot** (www.funspotnh. com), this resort town verges on the tacky but will be a hit with the kids. You can also board the **M/S Mount Washington** (tel: 603-366-5531; www. cruisenh.com; 2½-hour cruise), an elegant 1888 steamship (now diesel) that has served as a pleasure cruiser here

since 1940. The 200ft (60m) boat serenely threads its way past the lake's islands. Back on shore, there's a nice public beach at Endicott Park.

SQUAM LAKE

Continue north on Route 3 through the arty town of **Meredith** to **Squam Lake** ❸. **Holderness** is the main town here and, like Squam Lake itself, its image contrasts sharply with the tourist-oriented west shore of Winnipesaukee. This is the genteel, old-money summer milieu captured in the 1981 film *On Golden Pond*, which was filmed here. The **Squam Lakes Natural Science Center** (tel: 603-968-7194; www.nhnature.org; May–Nov daily 9.30am–4.30pm; charge) is a 200-acre (80ha) preserve, which features native wildlife in a woodland setting, trails, interactive exhibits, and animal programs.

CENTER SANDWICH

Follow Route 113, as it curves north then east, for 13 miles (21km) to the trim village of **Center Sandwich** ❹ (www.discoversandwich.com), where the **League of New Hampshire Craftsmen** (www.nhcrafts.org) was launched more than 70 years ago. The league's first store is at 32 Main Street (May–Oct Mon–Sat 10am–5pm, Sun noon–5pm), while across the street is the **Corner House Inn**, see 🍴②.

MOULTONBOROUGH

Follow Route 109 south for 4 miles (6km) to **Moultonborough** ❺, where the **Old Country Store** (1011 Whittier Highway; tel: 603-476-5750; www.nhcountrystore.com; daily 9am–6pm) has been selling necessities since it was built as a stagecoach stop in 1781, and has a small museum of artifacts to prove it.

Three miles (5km) from Moultonborough, off Route 109, is the **Castle in the Clouds** ❻ (Route 171; tel: 1-800-729-2468; www.castleintheclouds.org; mid-May–mid-June Sat–Sun 10am–4.30pm, mid-June–late Oct daily; charge). Shoe manufacturer Thomas G. Plant started to build this fantasy home made of granite in 1911, on a lofty site overlooking the Ossipee Mountains and miles of forest. Return to Route 109 for 17 miles (27km) back to Wolfeboro.

Above from far left: morning mist on Lake Winnipesaukee; Castle in the Clouds.

Lake Views
For great views of Lake Winnipesaukee, hike the 1½-mile (2.5km) trail to the 1,780ft (543m) summit of Mount Major, which is accessed off Route 11 to the northwest of Alton Bay.

Food and Drink 🍴

① GARWOODS
6 North Main Street, Wolfeboro; tel: 603-569-7788; www.garwoodsrestaurant.com; daily 11.30am–8.30pm; $$
A wood-beamed restaurant and pub, with a decent selection of food and deck seating beside the lake.

② CORNER HOUSE INN
22 Main Street, Center Sandwich; tel: 603-284-6219; www.cornerhouseinn.com; Mon, Wed–Thur 4.30–9pm, Fri–Sat 4.30–10pm, Sun 11.30am–2pm, mid-June–Sept daily 11.30am–2pm, 4.30–9pm; $–$$
This former inn and carriage house offers a good-value menu that takes in seafood, flatbread pizzas, and burgers, and includes locally sourced ingredients.

THE WHITE MOUNTAINS

Train enthusiasts and hikers will enjoy this loop drive through New Hampshire's picturesque White Mountains, which includes an ascent of Mount Washington – New England's highest point.

DISTANCE 109 miles (175km)

TIME Two days

START/END Conway

POINTS TO NOTE

This tour can be linked with New Hampshire's Lakes Region *(see p.80)*. Portland in Maine *(see p.88)* is 61 miles (98km) southeast.

Once the rugged frontier of New England, New Hampshire's White Mountains emerged as a tourist playground in the late 19th-century days of railroad travel and grand hotels, when the uplands provided a cool summer haven. Sections of the original railroad still see tourist trains today, while the 800,000-acre (325,000ha) White Mountain National Forest offers miles of unspoiled vistas, marvelous hiking terrain, and modern recreational facilities, including one of New England's most historic resorts.

KANCAMAGUS HIGHWAY

Named for a 17th-century Native American chief, the **Kancamagus Highway ❶** (Route 112) runs 26½

miles (43km) from just west of **Conway** to Lincoln. Passing through the White Mountain National Forest, the road constitutes one of New England's great scenic experiences, cresting the 2,860ft (872m), elevated **Kancamagus Pass**.

At the Lincoln end you will find the popular ski resort **Loon Mountain** (tel: 603-745-8111; www.loonmtn.com), and on the west side of I-93 in **North Woodstock**, the **Woodstock Inn**, see ⑪①. Just to the north on Route 3, kids will enjoy the mini theme park **Clark's Trading Post ❷** (no. 110; tel: 603-745-8913; www.clarkstradingpost. com; mid-May–mid-Oct, hours vary; charge), where attractions include a trained black-bear show, a climbing wall, and a 30-minute excursion on the White Mountain Central Railroad.

FRANCONIA NOTCH

From North Woodstock head north through the **Franconia Notch ❸** mountain pass. Apart from camping and hiking, the state park here contains several attractions, including **The Flume** (tel: 603-745-8391; www.visit nh.gov/flume; May–Oct daily 9am–5pm; charge), an 800ft (245m) glacially

---

Old Mountain Man
A cliffside along the along Franconia Notch was once home to the famed Old Man of the Mountains, a natural rock formation resembling a stern face. The ancient icon crashed to the valley below in 2002. It survives on the state's US quarter coin.

carved chasm through which a walkway follows a rushing stream and chain of waterfalls. The walk to and from the entrance takes around an hour.

Cannon Mountain Tramway
Farther up I-93, the **Cannon Mountain Aerial Tramway** (tel: 603-823-8800; www.cannonmt.com; June–Oct and Dec–mid-Apr daily 9am–5pm; charge) serves the Cannon Mountain ski area, providing sweeping views of the ranges.

Near the cable-car base, the **New England Ski Museum** (tel: 603-823-7177; www.skimuseum.org; mid-May–Mar 10am–5pm; free) displays evocative photos and antique equipment.

WHITE MOUNTAINS HIGHWAY

Turn off I-93 onto Route 302, the **White Mountains Highway**, to reach the resort town of **Bethlehem ④**, popular with allergy sufferers, who benefit from its pollen-free environment, and golfers, who enjoy the nearby courses.

Above from far left: view from Mount Willard; dog-sledding at the Mount Washington Resort.

Food and Drink

① WOODSTOCK INN
North Woodstock; tel: 603-745-3951; www.woodstockinnnh.com; daily 11.30am–10pm; $$
A super extensive menu and on-site microbrewery are the pluses at this Victorian country inn that incorporates the old Lincoln railway station.

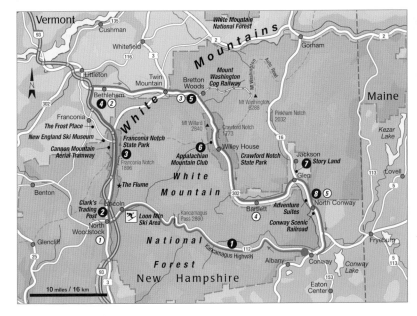

The Frost Place

Robert Frost (1874–1963) wrote some of his most famous poems at The Frost Place (tel: 603-823-5510; www.frostplace.org; July–mid-Oct Wed–Mon 1–5pm, May–June Sat–Sun; charge). There's a museum at what is now an educational center for poetry and the arts, as well as a nature trail on the grounds. To get there, drive 1 mile (1.5km) south of Franconia on Route 116. Turn left on Bickford Hill Road and left again on Ridge Road.

On the outskirts the **Adair County Inn** *(see p.112)* is a recommended place to stay, while in the heart of town itself **Marketplace at WREN** (2013 Main Street; tel: 603-869-3100; www.wrencommunity.org; daily 10am–5pm) showcases the craftwork of over 200 local artisans; next door is **Cold Mountain Café**, see ⑪②.

Bretton Woods and Mount Washington Resort

The highway leads up to Crawford Notch, the third mountain pass on this route, passing through the resort area of **Bretton Woods** ❺ on the way. Famous for being the location of a World War II conference, it is home to the historic **Mount Washington Hotel** *(see p.112)*, the sole survivor of several grand late 19th-century hotels that put the White Mountains on the summer vacation map.

Today the beautifully restored hotel is the focus of the **Mount Washington Resort** (tel: 1-800-258-0330; www.mountwashingtronresort.com), which not only includes facilities for skiers, golfers, horseback riders, and hikers, but also has a new spa and heated outdoor pool; drop by for afternoon tea if nothing else.

Reservations are essential for the resort's **Canopy Tour** (tel: 603-278-4947; charge), on which would-be action heroes can spend a thrilling three and a half hours traversing the mountain tops using 10 zip-lines, two sky bridges, and three rappels.

Mount Washington Cog Railway

Next to the resort restaurant, **Fabyan's Station**, see ⑪③, is the turnoff to the **Mount Washington Cog Railway** (tel: 603-278-5404; www.thecog.com; May–Oct, check website for times; charge), completed in 1869. Coal-fired steam locomotives still haul passengers up gradients so steep they are almost sheer to the 6,300ft (1,900m) peak; the round-trip, including a 20-minute stop at the summit, takes three hours.

At the top is the **Sherman Adams Summit Building** (tel: 603-466-3988; www.mountwashington.org), a fascinating institution that presents a history of weather; the world's highest

---

Mount Washington Road

There are a couple more ways of reaching the summit of Mount Washington other than on the Cog Railway. One is to hike there – a common route is from Pinkham Notch, the easternmost pass through the White Mountains, 10 miles (16km) north of Glen along Route 16. There's an Appalachian Mountain Club information and accommodation center there *(see also opposite)*, where staff can advise on trail routes.

Five miles (8km) farther north is the base station for the Mount Washington Auto Road (tel: 603-466-3988; www.mtwashingtonautoroad.com; early May–mid-Oct 9am–4pm; charge), which opened in 1861. The gradients of this 8-mile (13km) toll route to the summit reach 18 degrees. Always thrilling, the road is a highway to the clouds, and to magnificent views when they disperse. If you don't fancy driving up yourself, there are also guided tours.

Above: Mount Washington Cog Railway.

wind speed of 231mph (372kph) was recorded here in 1936.

Crawford Notch

Farther along the highway, near the crest of **Crawford Notch**, the **Appalachian Mountain Club ❻** (tel: 603-278-4453; www.outdoors.org) has built a handsome lodge, offering rooms, meals, and dormitory accommodations *(see p.112)*. Guided walks and outdoor gear (loaned for free) are also available here.

TOWARD NORTH CONWAY

Head down the highway, past the town of **Bartlett** and the **White Mountain Cider Company**, see ⑪④, toward **Glen**. Just to the north, on Route 16, is the theme park **Story Land ❼** (tel: 603-383-4293; www.storylandnh.com; May–Oct, check website for days and times; charge), with 21 family-friendly rides in a storybook setting. Now head south toward North Conway. On the north edge, the kids (and those in search of quirky accommodation) will want to stop at the **Adventure Suites** theme hotel *(see p.112)*.

Conway Scenic Railroad

From the row of shops and hotels that line the highway, it is clear that **North Conway ❽** is the commercial capital of White Mountains tourism. Try to time your arrival to coincide with one

of the departures along the **Conway Scenic Railroad** (tel: 603-356-5251; www.conwayscenic.com; June–Dec; charge). Trains leave from a Victorian station across the green in the town center. The railway offers the chance to have lunch or dinner in the Chocorua dining car. Alternatively, there is no shortage of places to eat here, including the **Stairway Café**, see ⑪⑤, opposite the station. It is 6 miles (9.5km) south to Conway.

Food and Drink

② COLD MOUNTAIN CAFÉ
2015 Main Street, Bethlehem; tel: 603-869-2500; www.coldmountaincafe.com; Mon–Sat 11am–9pm; $–$$
A pleasant café and gallery next to the Marketplace at WREN craft shop.

③ FABYAN'S STATION
Route 302, Bretton Woods; tel: 603-278-222; www.mountwashingtonresort.com; daily 11am–9pm; $$
Occupying the area's original railroad station, Fabyan's is the Mount Washington resort's casual dining option, serving chicken wings, burgers, soups, and salads. Look out for the toy train running on a track hanging from the ceiling.

④ WHITE MOUNTAIN CIDER COMPANY
Route 302, Bartlett; tel: 603-383-9061; www.whitemountaincider.com; deli daily 7am–5pm, restaurant Thur–Sat 5–9pm; $–$$$
Stop by this deli for cheap coffee, freshly made cider donuts and apple cider, as well as sandwiches. The evening restaurant in a rustic barn provides contemporary gourmet cuisine.

⑤ STAIRWAY CAFÉ
2649 Route 302, North Conway; tel: 603-356-5200; daily 7am–3pm; $–$$
A cute breakfast and lunch joint, with super colorful decor and a small terrace overlooking the town green and station.

PORTSMOUTH

History buffs, garden lovers, and foodies will love this meander around Portsmouth, one of New England's oldest settlements, where aspects of four centuries of American life are preserved and celebrated.

DISTANCE 2 miles (3.25km)

TIME A full day

START Strawbery Banke Museum

END John Paul Jones House

POINTS TO NOTE

Most of Portsmouth's sights are only open from June to mid-October. C&J (www.ridecj.com) runs a bus service (1½ hours) between Boston and Portmouth's transit centre, off I-95, from where a trolley bus (www.coastbus.org) will take you into town; a taxi is around $17. If you plan to spend the night, try the waterfront Ale House Inn *(see p.112)*. Portland, Maine *(see p.88)*, is 52 miles (84km) north via I-95.

Standing at the mouth of the Piscataqua River, and graced with a superb natural harbor, Portsmouth is the nation's third-oldest English settlement. Much of its 400-year history has been lovingly preserved in the downtown area, peppered with historic houses and their attendant gardens. Its many delicious dining options also make the compact town a fine destination for gourmets.

STRAWBERY BANKE

Pull into Hancock Street and park in front of the **Strawbery Banke Museum** ❶ (Marcy Street; tel: 603-433-1100; http://strawberybanke.org; May–Oct 10am–5pm; charge). This urban quarter of 42 preserved houses is Portsmouth's highlight. The English named their 1623 colony for the profusion of wild strawberries that greeted them; today, the 10-acre (4ha) living history museum tells the story of the city's oldest neighborhood from 1650 to 1950. Costumed guides and artisans make barrels and pottery, tend the lovely gardens, and keep up lively repartee in such roles as an immigrant Jewish woman from 1919. Dine later at **The Dunway Restaurant at Strawbery Banke** *(see p.118)*.

Food and Drink 🍴

① GENO'S CHOWDER & SANDWICH SHOP
177 Mechanic Street; tel: 603-427-2070; www.genoschowder.com; Mon–Sat 8.30am–4pm; $
This whitewashed, riverside cottage dishes up fish chowder and lobster rolls.

② THE FRIENDLY TOAST
121 Congress Street; tel: 603-430-2145; Mon–Thur 7am–midnight, Fri–Sat 24hrs, Sun 7am–9pm; $
This colorful diner is famous for its killer breakfasts and sandwiches.

Prescott Park

It is hard to believe that the genteel area of pretty cottages around Strawbery Banke was once Portsmouth's red light district. The efforts of the local Prescott sisters helped clean the area up, and it is for them that the nearby riverside **Prescott Park ②** is named. The Prescott Park Arts Festival (www.prescott park.org) is held here every summer.

HISTORIC HOUSES

Just south are two of Portsmouth's many historic house museums: **Wentworth-Gardner House** and **Tobias Lear House ③** (50 Mechanic Street; tel: 603-436-4006; www.wentworthgardner andlear.org; June–mid-Oct Thur–Sun noon–4pm; charge). In the former, a 1760 structure facing the Piscataqua River, are photographs by Wallace Nutting, a founder of the Colonial Revival movement. Nearby is **Geno's Chowder & Sandwich Shop**, see ⑪①.

Walk back past Prescott Park and turn left on Daniel Street to view the 1716 **Warner House ④** (no. 150; tel: 603-436-5909; www.warnerhouse.org; mid-June–mid-Oct Tue and Thur–Sat noon–4pm; charge). This was the first of Portsmouth's many brick houses, and sports a stairwell decorated with an array of early 18th-century murals.

Old warehouses transformed into restaurants and boutiques line Bow Street leading around to Market Street, where you will find the **Moffatt-Ladd House and Garden ⑤** (no. 54; tel: 603-436-8221; www.moffattladd.org; 1-hour tours mid-June–mid-Oct, Mon–Sat 11am–5pm, Sun 1–5pm; charge), an imposing three-story Georgian mansion topped with a captain's walk and graced with terraced English-style gardens.

Walk south along Market Street, turn right on Congress Street and left on Middle Street. More pretty gardens front the **John Paul Jones House ⑥** (no. 43; tel: 603-436-8420; www.ports mouthhistory.org; mid-May–mid-Oct Thur–Tue 11am–5pm; charge). The Revolutionary War naval hero once rented a room here.

Just on State Street is **Rockingham House**, where the treaty ending the 1905 Russo-Japanese War was signed (it now houses **The Library Restaurant**, see p.118). Back on Congress Street is **The Friendly Toast**, see ⑪②.

Above from far left: Portsmouth is sited on the Piscataqua; Strawbery Banke; tugboat in the harbor.

Isles of Shoals

For pleasant couple of hours' diversion, hop aboard one of the cruises offered by the Isles of Shoals Steamship Company (315 Market Street; tel: 1-800-441-4620; www.isleofshoals. com; charge) out to the rugged little archipelago lying 10 miles (16km) offshore.

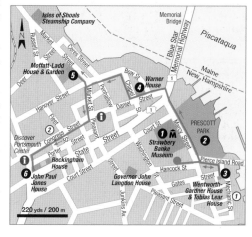

PORTLAND AND MIDCOAST MAINE

From the arty metropolis of Portland to the upscale sailing town of Camden, this route explores Midcoast Maine, taking in a genteel university town, quaint fishing villages, and the retail delights of Freeport.

> **DISTANCE** 87 miles (140km)
> **TIME** Two to three days
> **START** Portland
> **END** Camden
> **POINTS TO NOTE**
> For more information on Portland, see www.downtownportland.org. Amtrak's Downeaster train service (www.amtrakdowneaster.com) connects Boston with Portland. Castine, start of the Down East Maine tour *(see p.92),* is 54 miles (87km) north around the coast.

PORTLAND

There's a gritty urban vibe to **Portland ❶**, Maine's largest city, where you will find revived, 19th-century red-brick and stone warehouses and buildings in the Old Port District, cutting-edge art galleries, and a host of gastronomic delights. It is the kind of place where tattooed teens skateboard through town once the evening traffic has died down, and where the waterfront is an atmospheric place to hang on a warm summer evening.

Portland Museum of Art

Begin at the **Portland Museum of Art ❹** (7 Congress Square; tel: 207-775-6148; www.portlandmuseum.org; Tue–Sun 10am–5pm, Fri until 9pm, mid-May–mid-Oct also Mon 10am–5pm; charge, Fri 5–9pm free), the nucleus around which many small commercial galleries gravitate. Maine's largest public art institution offers nicely sized galleries containing an eclectic collection that spans three centuries of American art by the likes of Andrew Wyeth, Winslow Homer, and Andy Warhol, as well as works by European masters, such as Renoir, Monet, and Picasso. A highlight is the McLellan House, a beautifully preserved townhouse from 1801, attached to the main galleries.

Wadsworth Longfellow House

From the art museum it's a five-minute walk down Congress Street, past the outstanding restaurant **Five Fiftyfive** *(see p.119)* to **Wadsworth Longfellow House ❸** (no. 489; tel: 207-774-1822; www.mainehistory.org; May–Oct Mon–Sat 10.30am–4pm, Sun noon–4pm; charge), childhood home of Portland's

most famous literary son *(see also p.42)*. Guided tours are conducted around the 1785 brick house – Portland's oldest such structure – as well as its restored Colonial Revival garden.

Old Port District

Portland owes much of its present-day distinction to the transformation of its dilapidated waterfront district into the **Old Port District ⓒ** (roughly bounded by Middle, Union, and Commerical streets). This buzzing neighborhood is packed with crafts shops, boutiques, cafés, and restaurants: try **Duckfat**, see ⓖⓘ, at the far end of Middle Street for lunch, and **Bresca** and **Fore Street** *(see p.119)* for dinner. For beer brewed on the premises, head to **Gritty Mc-Duff's Brew Pub** *(see p.123)*.

Victoria Mansion

Return toward the art museum along Park Street and you will pass **Victoria Mansion ⓓ** (109 Danforth Street; tel: 207-772-4841; www.victoriamansion. org; May–Oct Mon–Sat 10am–4pm, Sun 1–5pm; charge), one of America's most extravagant Victorian homes. Built in 1859, its sedate brownstone facade belies a riotously ornate interior.

FREEPORT

Drive 17 miles (27km) northeast out of Portland on Route 1 to **Freeport ❷**, New England's most famous outlet-mall (discounted brand-name goods)

town. The many outlet stores *(see p.19)* that line the streets arrived in the wake of **L.L. Bean** (95 Main Street; www. llbean.com; daily 24hrs). Founded in 1912 by Leon Leonwood Bean as a purveyor of the waterproof hunting boots (still a mainstay), it sells just about everything related to the outdoors. There's a café in the huge complex, as well as a kiosk for **Linda Bean's Perfect Maine Lobster Rolls**, see ⓖ② *(p.90)*.

Food and Drink

① **DUCKFAT**
43 Middle Street, Portland; tel: 207-774-8080; www.duck fat.com; Mon–Sat 11am–9pm, Sun 11am–5pm; $–$$
Portlanders are rightly crazy for the yummy Belgian-style frites with truffle ketchup that accompany panini sandwiches: try the duck confit one.

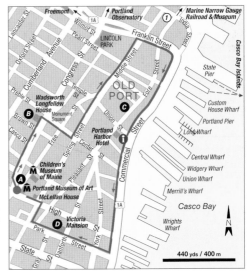

Food and Drink

② LINDA BEAN'S PERFECT MAINE LOBSTER ROLLS
57 Main Street, Freeport; tel: 207-865-1874; www.linda beansperfectmaine.com; daily 11am–6pm; $
Check out Linda's claim to the ideal roll at this takeaway kiosk on the corner of Main and Morse streets.

③ MAE'S CAFÉ AND BAKERY
160 Centre Street, Bath; tel: 207-442-8577; www.maescafeandbakery.com; daily 8am–3pm; $–$$
Drop by this convivial place for delicious baked goods, breakfast dishes, sandwiches, and other light meals.

④ RED'S EATS
41 Water Street, Wiscasset; tel: 207-882-6128; Apr–Sept daily 11am–9pm; $
This quintessential Maine food shack has been dishing up fantastic lobster rolls and clams since the 1940s.

⑤ ROCKLAND CAFÉ
441 Main Street, Rockland; tel: 207-596-7556; www.rocklandcafe.com; daily 5.30am–9.30pm; $–$$
Try the homemade fish cakes and other good-value seafood dishes at this unfussy, friendly diner.

Cruising the Islands

The peninsulas and islands off Maine's coast are best seen from the decks of a wooden windjammer. The schooners *Heritage* (tel: 207-594-8007; www.schoonerheritage.com) and *Victory Chimes* (tel: 1-800-745-5651; www.victorychimes.com) both sail out of Rockland. Alternatively, the Maine State Ferry (tel: 800-491-4883; www.state.me.us/mdot/opt/ferry/maine-ferry-service.php) goes to Vinalhaven and North Haven, serene islands with tidy villages overlooking Penobscot Bay.

The Monhegan Boat Line (tel: 207-372-8848; www.monheganboat.com) connects Port Clyde (10 miles/16km south of Rockland via Route 73) with the island of Monhegan, which features 17 miles (27km) of hiking trails.

BRUNSWICK

Ten miles (16km) farther along Route 1 is **Brunswick ❸**, home of prestigious **Bowdoin College**, founded in 1794. Two alumni, explorers Admiral Robert E. Peary and Captain Donald MacMillan, are remembered at the **Peary-MacMillan Arctic Museum** (Hubbard Hall; tel: 207-725-3416; www.bowdoin.edu/arctic-museum; Tue–Sat 10am–5pm, Sun 2–5pm; donation). Here you will find photos, documents, and equipment from their polar expeditions.

The **Bowdoin Museum of Art** (Walker Building; tel: 207-725-3275; www.bowdoin.edu/art-museum; Tue–Sat 10am–5pm, Thur until 8.30pm, Sun 1–5pm; donation), which has benefited from a recent $20 million renovation, exhibits works by American colonial, Impressionist, and modern painters, as well as by European masters.

BATH

Continue along Route 1 to the ship-building town of **Bath ❹**, where the **Maine Maritime Museum and Shipyard** (243 Washington Street; tel: 207-443-1316; www.mainemaritimemuseum.org; daily 9.30am–5pm; charge), set in 25 acres (10ha) on the banks of the Kennebec River, chronicles the industry that still keeps the town's economy ticking. Grab refreshments in town at **Mae's Café and Bakery**, see ⑪③.

WISCASSET

The next stop, 9 miles (14km) farther along Route 1, is the picturesque village of **Wiscasset ⑤**, known for its elegant Federal-style homes and numerous antiques shops. The grand mansion **Castle Tucker** (2 Lee Street; tel: 207-882-7169; www.historicnew england.org; June–mid-Oct Wed–Sun 11am–4pm; charge) overlooks the Sheepscot River from atop a hill at one end of town and is worth going up to just for the view. Back down by the river, next to the bridge across the inlet, enjoy a lobster roll from **Red's Eats**, see ⑪④.

ROCKLAND

Continue along Route 1 for 42 miles (68km) to reach **Rockland ⑥**, one of Midcoast's less prettified towns, which has, nonetheless, been making a name for itself lately as a destination for art lovers and foodies. The Maine Lobster Festival (www.mainelobsterfestival. com) is held here at the end of July, and Rockland's working harbor is the jumping-off point for cruises and ferries to and around nearby islands *(see feature, opposite)*.

The town's **Farnsworth Art Museum** (16 Main Street; tel: 207-596-6457; www.farnsworthmuseum.org; 9am–5pm; charge) has an excellent American collection, and is strong on paintings by the Wyeth family. After touring it, settle down for lunch at **Rockland Café**, see ⑪⑤, or dinner at **Primo** *(see p.119)*.

CAMDEN

Enjoying a spectacular bayside location, **Camden ⑦**, 8 miles (13km) north of Rockland, is an ideal base for touring the Midcoast. The town's snowy white captains' mansions attest to its seafaring prosperity.

For the best panoramic view of Camden and surrounding waters, head to **Camden Hills State Park** (tel: 207-236-3109; www.state.me.us; mid-May–mid-Oct dawn–dusk; charge) and hike or drive to the summit of the 800ft (245m) **Mount Battie**.

Above from far left: lobster-fishing; Rockland's harbor; looking out over Camden from Mount Battie.

Eastern Railroad
The Maine Eastern Railroad (tel: 866-637-2457; www.maine easternrailroad.com; May–Oct) offers train excursions between Brunswick and Rockland, with stops in Bath and Wiscasset and scenic coastal views along the way.

Transportation Museum
Two miles (3.25km) south of Rockland, transport enthusiasts and kids may enjoy the Owls Head Transportation Museum (Route 73; tel: 207-594-4418; www. ohtm.org; daily 10am–5pm; charge), packed with antique cars and airplanes; it also hosts weekend air shows.

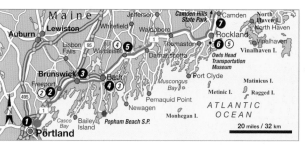

DOWN EAST MAINE

This beautiful, remote region is Maine at its most picturesque and rugged. Drive through attractive coastal villages to the Acadia National Park, with its granite headlands, upland meadows, pine forests, and thundering surf.

Down East

The term 'Down East' for Maine's far northern reaches came into fashion in the 19th century, when southern New England relied on lumber shipped from here.

DISTANCE 52 miles (84km) from Castine to Bar Harbor

TIME Two to three days

START Castine

END Bar Harbor

POINTS TO NOTE

Bangor Airport (www.flybangor. com) is 47 miles (76km) north of Castine. Alternatively, follow on from Midcoast Maine *(see p.88)*.

CASTINE

From Orland on Route 1, head south for 14 miles (23km) via routes 175 and 166 to begin the tour at the pretty village of **Castine** ❶ (www.castine.me.us), perched on a peninsula near the head of Penobscot Bay. The ruins of **Fort George** (Battle Avenue) are a reminder of its historic past; the British occupied Castine during the Revolution. More than a century before that, the French had set up a trading post here.

Today, students train at the prestigious **Maine Maritime Academy**, and tourists wander the neat grid of streets lined with Federal and Greek Revival structures, several of which are now guesthouses and restaurants: check out **The Castine Inn** *(see p.113)*, which has lovely gardens, and the **Pentagöet Inn** *(see p.119)*, which serves delicious food.

Park Information

The Hulls Cove Visitor Center (tel: 207-667-8550; mid-May–Oct 8am–4.30pm) will help you plan your visit to Acadia National Park, with its 15-minute orientation video and information about ranger-led walks and camping.

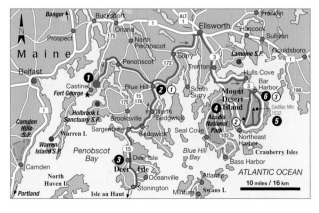

BLUE HILL AND DEER ISLE

Twenty miles (32km) east of Castine, via routes 175 and 177, is the equally attractive town of **Blue Hill ❷** (www.bluehillme.com), known for its galleries and crafts shops displaying the works of local artists. Drop by **Leighton Gallery** (24 Parker Point Road; tel: 207-374-5001; www.leightongallery.com; Mon–Sat 10.30am–5pm, Sun noon–5pm), which has a sculpture garden, and the **Blue Hill Co-Op Community Market and Café**, see ⓘⓘ①.

At this point you could drive south to Sargentville, where a causeway leads to **Deer Isle ❸**. From the fishing village of **Stonington** at the southernmost tip, you can take a ferry (tel: 207-367-5193; www.isleauhaut.com; charge) to tranquil **Isle au Haut**. Part of this rocky island falls within Acadia National Park and is threaded with hiking trails.

ACADIA NATIONAL PARK

Accessible via causeway from Route 3, and about 24 miles (38km) from Blue Hill, much of **Mount Desert Island** is covered by the beautiful and popular **Acadia National Park ❹** (tel: 207-288-3338; www.nps.gov/acad; May–Oct; charge). John D. Rockefeller Jr donated 10,000 acres (4,000ha) to the park and ordered the construction of the island's 58 miles (93km) of gravel-topped carriage roads, enjoyed today by hikers and mountain bikers.

Within the park, **Cadillac Mountain ❺**, at 1,532ft (467m), is the highest point on the East Coast and the first place in the nation to greet the sun's morning rays. You can drive to the summit on a spur off the 20-mile (32km) loop road that passes other park highlights including **Sand Beach** and **Thunder Hole**. Drop by **Jordan Pond House**, see ⓘⓘ②, for refreshments.

Facing Frenchman Bay, bustling **Bar Harbor ❻** has attracted vacationers and the sailing crowd since the 19th century. Climb aboard Captain John's **Lulu Lobster Boat Ride** (56 West Street; tel: 207-963-2341; www.lululobsterboat.com; daily May–Oct; charge) for a two-hour insight into the local lobster fishing industry. You could eat at **2 Cats**, see ⓘⓘ③, or **Café This Way** *(see p.119)*.

Above from far left: Acadia National Park; Sand Beach.

Abbe Museum
The state's native people, the Wabanaki, are celebrated in Bar Harbor at the Abbe Museum Downtown (2 Mount Desert Street; tel: 207-288-3519; http://abbemuseum.org; mid-May–early Nov daily 10am–6pm, rest of year Thur–Sat 10am–4pm; charge), with an extensive collection of tribal artifacts and spaces for quiet reflection.

Food and Drink

① BLUE HILL CO-OP COMMUNITY MARKET AND CAFÉ
4 Ellsworth Road, Blue Hill; tel: 207-374-2165; www.bluehill.coop; daily 7am–9pm; $
Fair-trade coffee, sandwiches, baked goods, and many other tasty products are available at this gem of a store.

② JORDAN POND HOUSE
Park Loop Road, Acadia National Park; tel: 207-276-3316; www.jordanpond.com; daily mid-May–Oct 11.30am–8pm; $$
Pause for lunch or afternoon tea at this rest-house overlooking the water and surrounded by mountains and forest.

③ 2 CATS
130 Cottage Street, Bar Harbor; tel: 207-288-2808; www.2catsbarharbor.com; daily 7am–1pm; $–$$
A cute-as-can-be café and inn (it has three rooms for rent) that specializes in breakfast dishes.

DIRECTORY

A user-friendly alphabetical listing of practical information, plus hand-picked hotels and restaurants, clearly organised by area, to suit all budgets and tastes. Select nightlife listings are also included here.

A

AGE RESTRICTIONS

The age of consent is 16 throughout New England, and you have to be 21 to drink legally in each of the six states. To drive, you need to be 16 in Connecticut, Vermont, and Maine, 17 in New Hampshire, and 18 in Massachusetts and Rhode Island.

B

BUDGETING

It will cost around $7 for a beer or a glass of house wine. A main course at a budget restaurant runs to around $10, at a moderate one $25, and at an expensive one over $25. Budget, moderate, and deluxe accommodations are under $75, between $75–200, and over $200, respectively. A taxi from Boston's Logan Airport to a hotel in the Back Bay area will cost around $25. Single bus and subway tickets in Boston cost $1.50 and $2, but are reduced to $1.25 and $1.70 if you buy a Charlie Card (see p.105).

C

CHILDREN

It is easy to travel in New England with kids. There are hands-on museums, state and theme parks, and toy- and bookstores throughout the region; and, with good planning, driving distances between destinations can be kept relatively short. Note that laws in each state are quite specific about driving with children in a car. Be sure to tell the car-rental agency in advance how old your children are, so that they will have the proper-size car seats available, and check with them about state requirements.

Many restaurants offer kids' menus, but some – particularly more expensive ones – may not welcome young children at dinner. Lodgings generally welcome children, and do not charge for those under 18, although $10 or $15 may be added to the bill for a cot or crib.

CLOTHING

In winter, warm clothes and waterproof shoes are a must. For all other seasons, assume that you will encounter at least one cool spell, and carry a sweater or light jacket. Raingear is advisable, particularly in spring. For climate information, see pp.10–11.

Like the rest of the US, New England has grown increasingly less formal over the past few years, and casual clothing will see you through most situations. However, shorts, jeans, and T-shirts are still frowned upon in many of the better restaurants, particularly in cities; the finest Boston establishments – as well as a few traditional mountain, seaside, and lake resorts – still expect jackets (and, in a few cases, ties) for men. A neat pair of khakis together with a

blazer is virtually fail-safe; women should not encounter any problems with a casual dress or pantsuit.

CRIME AND SAFETY

Boston is one of the safest cities in the US, but visitors should always be vigilant. Areas where crime is a problem offer few tourist attractions and are on the fringes of the city. Equally, New England's urban areas are among the safest in the US. Nevertheless, always lock car doors, and don't leave valuables visible in your car or hotel room.

CUSTOMS

Anyone over 21 may bring 200 cigarettes, 50 cigars, or 3lbs of tobacco, 1 liter of alcohol, and a maximum of $100 worth of duty-free gifts. Importing meat products, seeds, plants, or fruits is illegal, as are narcotics. You may take out anything you wish, but consult with the authorities of your destination country for its customs regulations on entry.

D

DISABLED TRAVELERS

Boston caters well to the disabled traveler, with accessible bathrooms and ramps on public buildings, curbsides, and at most attractions. However, it is also an old city with colonial buildings and cobblestone sidewalks, so despite

best efforts it is not always perfect. Check the Massachusetts Bay Transit Authority's website (www.mbta.com) for public transport access information for disabled travelers, including details of its The Ride service for door-to-door paratransit. For more information, call tel: 617-222-3200 or TTY 617-222-5146. Boston's Commission for Persons with Disabilities can be reached on tel: 617-635-3682 or via www.cityofboston.gov/civilrights/disability.asp.

Elsewhere in New England the situation is similar. Consult Access Able (www.access-able.com), Mobility International USA (www.miusa.org), and the Society for Accessible Travel & Hospitality (www.sath.org).

E

ELECTRICITY

The US uses 110–120V, 60-cycle AC voltage (as opposed to the 220–240V, 50-cycle of Europe). Laptops and many travel appliances are dual-voltage and will work, but check first. An adapter will be needed for US sockets.

EMBASSIES AND CONSULATES

Most embassies are based in Washington, DC, but many countries have consulates in Boston; a complete list can be found at www.state.gov/s/cpr/rls/dpl/32122.htm.

Above from far left: Bostix booth for discount theatre tickets in Boston *(see p.22)*; go Red Sox!; Boston motorbike cop.

Australia (embassy): 1601 Massachusetts Avenue, Washington, DC; tel: 202-797-3000; www.usa.embassy.gov.au.

Consulates in Boston
Canada: 3 Copley Place, Suite 400; tel: 617-262-3760; www.boston.gc.ca.
Ireland: 535 Boylston Street; tel: 617-267-9330; www.embassyofireland.org.
UK: 1 Memorial Drive, Suite 1500; tel: 617-245-4500; www.britainusa.com/boston.

EMERGENCY NUMBER

Ambulance, Fire, and Police: tel: 911.

GAY TRAVELERS

Massachusetts is famous as the first US state to legalize same-sex marriage. In general, Boston is a very integrated city, so you will find gays and straights mingling in many city neighborhoods. The South End has the highest concentration of gay bars and is also the home of the annual Boston Pride parade. The Greater Boston Business Council (www.gbbc.org) has information on businesses owned, operated, or supported by the local gay community.

Northampton in Massachusetts emerged as a lively enclave for lesbians in the late 20th century, and Provincetown on Cape Cod has long been one of the country's best-known gay summer vacation spots. You will also find sizeable gay communities and bars in Providence and Portland.

Bay Windows (www.baywindows.com) is a free weekly newspaper covering gay news, culture, and nightlife in Boston and New England. There's also www.outinboston.com and www.edgenewengland.com.

GREEN ISSUES

While many urban centers in New England practice recycling, the six states have a patchy record when it comes to environmental protection; the needs of industry and commerce have often trumped green considerations. The Conservation Law Foundation works to solve the most pressing environmental problems facing New England; its achievements have included protecting the Georges Bank from oil drilling and overfishing, ending decades of sewage dumping into Boston Harbor, preserving Vermont's bear habitats, and saving New Hampshire's Franconia Notch from a four-lane highway. For carbon-offsetting your trip, *see margin, opposite.*

HEALTH AND MEDICAL CARE

Sunburn will be the most common medical nuisance for most visitors.

Even so, don't leave home without travel insurance to cover yourself and your belongings. It is not cheap to get sick in the United States.

Pharmacies. These stock most standard medication (although some painkillers that are available over the counter in other countries may be prescription-only in the US), and staff are trained to help with most minor ailments. Across New England you will find branches of the pharmacy CVS (www.cvs.com). A central one in Boston is: 587 Boylston Street; tel: 617-437-8414.

Hospitals. These are signposted on highways with a white H on a blue background. Major hospitals have 24-hour emergency rooms; you may have a long wait before you get to see the doctor, but the care and treatment are thorough and professional.

Walk-in clinics are commonplace in cities, where you can consult a nurse or doctor for a minor ailment without an appointment. If cost is a concern, turn first to clinics offering free or pro-rated care (look then up in the Yellow Pages).

Major hospitals include:

Connecticut: Hartford Hospital, 80 Seymour Street; tel: 860-545 5000; www.harthosp.org.

Maine: Maine Medical Center, 22 Bramhall Street, Portland; tel: 207-662-0111; www.mmc.org.

Massachusetts: Massachusetts General Hospital, 55 Fruit Street, Boston; tel: 617-726-2000; www.massgeneral.org.

New Hampshire: Portsmouth Regional Hospital, 333 Borthwick Avenue; tel: 603-436-5110.

Rhode Island: Rhode Island Hospital, 593 Eddy Street, Providence; tel: 401-444-4000; wwwwww.nwcr.ws/rih.

Vermont: Fletcher Allen Medical Center Campus, 111 Colchester Avenue, Burlington; tel: 802-847-0000; www.fletcherallen.org.

HOURS AND HOLIDAYS

Most offices open Mon–Fri 9am–5pm. Federal and local government offices usually open Mon–Fri 8.30am–4.30pm. Banks open Mon–Fri 9am–4pm. Some also open until 5pm on Thur and Sat 9am–noon.

Public Holidays

All government offices, banks, and post offices are closed on public holidays. Public transportation does not run as often on these days, but most shops, museums, and attractions are open.

Jan 1 – New Year's Day
Third Mon Jan – Martin Luther King Day
Third Mon Feb – President's Day
Mar/Apr – Easter Sunday
Third Mon Apr – Patriot's Day
Last Mon May – Memorial Day
July 4 – Independence Day
First Mon Sept – Labor Day
Second Mon Oct – Columbus Day
Last Thur and Fri Nov – Thanksgiving
Dec 25 – Christmas

Carbon-Offsetting
Air travel produces a huge amount of carbon dioxide and is a significant contributor to global warming. If you would like to offset the damage caused to the environment by your flight, a number of organizations can do this for you using online 'carbon calculators' that tell you how much you need to donate. In the UK travelers can visit www.climatecare. org or www.carbon neutral.com; in the US log on to www. climatefriendly.com or www.sustainable travelinternational.org.

Magazines
The Boston Phoenix (www.thephoenix. com), a free weekly paper, includes the largest entertainment listings; there are also Portland and Providence versions. Another free weekly in Boston is the *Weekly Dig* (www.weekly dig.com). Out in western Massachusetts, the *Valley Advocate* (www. valleyadvocate.com) is a great resource for Pioneer Valley.

Useful monthly magazines include *Boston Magazine* (www.bostonmaga zine.com), *Yankee* (www.yankeemaga zine.com), and the Maine-focused *Down East* (www. downeast.com).

I

INTERNET

Throughout New England wireless internet access is ubiquitous in cafés, many student-type hangouts, and plenty of hotels and guesthouses. Many places charge an hourly rate, but you can also find free hotspots (www.ilove freewifi.com) throughout the region, and most public libraries allow free access via their computer terminals.

L

LEFT LUGGAGE

Security concerns in recent years have resulted in left-luggage facilities being closed in places such as bus and train stations. Your best option is to ask whether you can leave luggage at your hotel.

LOST PROPERTY

Most establishments operate their own lost-and-found department, but if you lose something in a public area, go to the local police station in the event it was turned in.

Lost or stolen credit cards:
Amex: tel: 1-800-528-2121
Diners Club/Carte Blanche: tel: 1-800-234-6377
MasterCard: tel: 1-800-307-7309
Visa: tel: 1-800-336-8472

M

MAPS

Insight Guides' *FlexiMap Boston* is laminated for durability and easy folding, and contains travel information as well as exceptionally clear cartography. For driving, try *The American Map New England Road Atlas* (www.americanmap.com).

MEDIA

Newspapers. As well as the US nationals, such as *USA Today* and the financial *Wall Street Journal*, New England has many local newspapers, including *The Boston Globe* (www. boston.com), *Boston Herald* (www. bostonherald.com), *Hartford Courant* (www.courant.com), *Portland Press Herald* (http://pressherald.mainetoday. com), and *Burlington Free Press* (www. burlingtonfreepress.com). *The Christian Science Monitor* (www.csmonitor. com), a prestigious newspaper published in Boston on weekdays, is strong on international news, and throughout New England you will be able to get hold of copies of *The New York Times* (www.nytimes.com).

For magazines, *see margin, left.*

Television. Most hotels receive the three major national networks (ABC, CBS, and NBC), many cable networks including CNN, Fox, and ESPN

(sports), and several premium movie channels, including HBO. The Public Broadcasting System (PBS) has some of the better-quality programs.

Radio. AM radio is geared toward talk, news, and information programming. FM stations tend to offer specific music formats, such as country or classic rock. Red Sox games are broadcast on over 60 stations throughout New England, anchored in Boston by WRKO-680 AM (www.wrko.com) and WEEI-850 AM (www.weei.com). New England Patriots games are aired on WBCN-104.1 FM (www.wbcn. com). National Public Radio (www. npr.org), known for in-depth news coverage, classical music, and special programing, has affiliates throughout New England.

MONEY

Major credit and debit cards are widely accepted. Some smaller restaurants may accept cash only; they will usually post this in the menu, or you can check with your waiter beforehand. Car-rental agencies and some hotels will require you to have a credit card. ATMs are plentiful. Traveler's checks are easily converted to cash at any bank, but you will need your passport to prove your identity. Foreign currency exchange is not handled by all banks; your best bets for this are travel services companies.

P

POST

Post offices are usually open Mon–Fri 8am–5pm, Sat 8am–noon. In Boston, the main post office is at 25 Dorchester Street (behind South Station; tel: 617-654-5302; www.usps.gov; daily 24 hours). Mail may be addressed to General Delivery at any post office; make sure the zip code is included in the address. At time of printing, it cost 98¢ to send a postcard or a letter to Europe.

S

SMOKING

The legal age in New England to buy tobacco is 18. Smoking is banned in most indoor public places and on transport. Some states ban smoking in restaurants; others specify non-smoking areas. Hotels have non-smoking rooms; many inns and B&Bs ban smoking.

T

TELEPHONES

Phone numbers. All telephone numbers have 10 digits. If you are calling outside the local area then a 1 precedes the 10-digit number.

The Greater Boston area code, included in the number even when calling within the city, is 617. Surrounding

towns use 508 (Plymouth and Provincetown), 781 (Lexington and Concord), and 978 (Salem and Cape Ann).

Four states in New England have one code each: Maine (207), New Hampshire (603), Rhode Island (401), and Vermont (802). In Connecticut, Hartford numbers are preceded by 860, those for New Haven by 203. Check all other locations in the directory.

Numbers beginning with codes 800 or 888 are toll-free if dialed within the US.

Calling from abroad. To contact the US from the UK, dial 00 (international code) + 1 (US) + a 10-digit number. For calls to other countries from the US, dial the international access code (011), then the country code, city code, and local number. Directory assistance is 555-1212 preceded by 1 and the area code you are calling from or inquiring about; so for Boston dial 1-617-555-1212.

Cellphones. The popularity of cellphones means that you will find few public telephone booths across New England. Newer handsets from Europe and Asia work in US cities, but reception in suburban and rural areas tends to be patchy. This is improving as the US upgrades its cell infrastructure. Pay-as-you-go SIMS that will work in your phone, depending on the model, can be purchased from outlets throughout the region. Main companies are AT&T (www.att.com), Sprint (www.sprint.com), and Verizon (www.verizon.com).

City Tourist Card

The Boston Card (tel: 1-800-887-9103; www.go bostoncard.com) is a one-, two-, three-, five-, or seven-day visitor pass, which offers unlimited admission to more than 60 attractions and tours in and around Boston. Cards can be bought online or at the Bostix booths at Faneuil Hall and Copley Square, and the Boston Common and Prudential Center visitor information centers.

TIME ZONES

All of New England is on Eastern Standard Time: three hours ahead of Los Angeles, one hour ahead of Chicago, five hours behind London, and 15 hours behind Tokyo. New England is one hour behind the Canadian provinces of New Brunswick and Nova Scotia. Daylight Saving Time is in effect between specified dates in early April and early November; turn clocks ahead one hour in spring, back one hour in fall.

TIPPING

Tipping is voluntary, but waiters, taxi drivers, bartenders etc will all expect a gratuity amounting to 15 percent of the bill, or 20 percent for above-average service. On restaurant checks over $100, a 20 percent tip is the norm. Tips are not included in restaurant checks, except for big parties; when calculating, do not tip on tax. Doormen, skycaps (airport porters), and porters receive about $1 per bag.

TOURIST INFORMATION

Connecticut Commission on Culture & Tourism, 2nd floor, 1 Constitution Plaza, Hartford; tel: 860-256-280/1-888-288-4748; www.ctvisit.com.
Maine Office of Tourism, 59 State House Station, Augusta; tel: 1-888-624-6345; www.visitmaine.com.

Massachusetts Office of Travel and Tourism, 10 Park Plaza, Suite 4510, Boston; tel: 617-973-8500/1-800-227-6277; www.massvacation.com.

New Hampshire Office of Travel & Tourism Development, 172 Pembroke Road, Concord; tel: 603-271-2665/1-800-386-4664; www.visitnh.gov.

Rhode Island Tourism Division, 315 Iron Horse Way, Providence; tel: 1-800-250-7384; www.visitrhode island.com.

Vermont Department of Tourism & Marketing, 6th floor, National Life Building, Montpelier; tel: 802-828-3237; www.vermontvacation.com.

Boston and Cambridge

The **Greater Boston Convention & Visitors Bureau** (2 Copley Place; tel: 617-536-4100/1-888-733-2678; www.bostonusa.com) runs two visitor centers: **Boston Common Visitor Information Center**, 148 Tremont Street; daily 9am–5pm (the booth here marks the start of the Freedom Trail).

Prudential Visitor Center, Center Court, Prudential Center, 800 Boylston Street; Mon–Sat 9am–5pm, Sun 1–5pm.

The **Cambridge Office of Tourism** (4 Brattle Street; tel: 1-800-862-5678/617-441-2884; www.cambridge-usa.org; Mon–Sat 9am–5pm) has a booth in the center of Harvard Square (tel: 617-497-1630; Mon–Sat 9am–5pm, Sun 11am–5pm).

TRANSPORTATION

Arrival by Air

Boston's **Logan Airport** (tel: 1-800-235-6426, www.massport.com), the main access point for international travelers to New England, has five terminals (A to E). Airlines do not necessarily use the same terminal for domestic and international flights. There are free wheelchair-lift-equipped shuttle buses that run between the terminals.

Regional airports include:

Bradley International, Windsor Locks, Connecticut; tel: 860-292-2000; www.bradleyairport.com.

Portland International Jetport, Portland, Maine; tel: 207-774-7301; www.portlandjetport.org.

Manchester Boston Regional Airport, 1 Airport Road, Manchester, New Hampshire; tel: 603-624-6556; www.flymanchester.com.

T. F. Green Airport, 2000 Post Road, Warwick, Rhode Island; tel: 401-737-400; www.pvdairport.com.

Burlington International Airport, Airport Drive, South Burlington, Vermont; tel: 802-863-1889; www.burlingtonintlairport.com.

Arrival by Land

By train. Amtrak (tel: 1-800-872-7245; www.amtrak.com) operates several routes that serve major New England cities and points in between. Boston's South Station is the north terminus of Amtrak's Northeast Corridor, linking

Other Air Options
Each state also has several smaller airports, most with limited commuter service. Visitors to southern parts of New England often choose to fly into one of the major New York City area airports – Kennedy, La Guardia, or Newark – and continue their travels via rail, bus, or rental car.

Tourist Websites
For general tourist information about New England, see www.visitnew england.com and www.discovernew england.org.

the city with New York and Washington, DC, via Providence and New Haven; trains – including the high-speed, extra-fare Acela – run frequently every day. The Lake Shore Limited runs daily between Boston and Chicago, with stops at Worcester and Springfield, Massachusetts. The Downeaster connects Boston's North Station with Portland, Maine. The Vermonter operates daily between Washington, DC, and St Albans, Vermont, via New York City, Hartford, Springfield, and major Vermont cities and towns. The Ethan Allen Express runs between New York and Rutland, Vermont.

By bus. Greyhound (tel: 1-800 231 2222; www.greyhound.com) and its regional affiliates serve major population centers and in-between points throughout New England, and link the region with its terminals in New York, Montreal, and points south and west.

By car. New England is well served by the US Interstate Highway system. I-95, the coastal artery, connects New York with New Haven, Providence, Boston, and Portland. East–west I-84 links southern New York State with eastern Massachusetts via Hartford. The Massachusetts Turnpike (I-90) joins the New York Thruway near Albany. North–south I-89 crosses into Vermont from Quebec southeast of Montreal, and links with Boston-bound I-93 at Concord, New Hampshire. North–

south I-91 runs between New Haven and the Vermont-Quebec border.

Within New England

Driving. New England is best traveled by automobile. In addition to the Interstate Highway system, the region is served by an excellent system of secondary federal and state highways, and county and municipal roads. Roads are generally well maintained, with every effort made to remove snow promptly; but in rural areas you might encounter miles of unpaved roads that can be tricky in winter or in the mud season that arrives with the spring thaw.

Road signs can cause problems even for experienced locals – you won't have trouble on major routes, but you may feel abandoned on some secondary roads. It is always a good idea to travel with detailed maps or GPS.

The speed limit on Interstate Highways in New England is 65mph (105kph), except in urban areas where it is 55mph (90kph). On secondary highways in rural areas it is usually 50mph (80kph). In built-up areas you must slow to 20–40mph (32–64kph); city speed limits rarely exceed 25mph (40 kph). Look out for signs – limits can change abruptly, especially on the outskirts of towns. A right turn on a red traffic signal is permissible after a complete stop anywhere in New England, except where there is a No Turn on Red sign. At a rotary (roundabout), yield to vehicles already in it.

Car rental. Major US car-rental firms are represented at Boston's Logan Airport, as well as at smaller airports and city locations throughout New England. Note that drivers must be 21 to rent a car, and that rental agreements may forbid taking a car rented in New England to New York or New Jersey without payment of a surcharge. Children under the age of five or under 40lbs (18kg) must be protected by a child safety seat, available at extra cost.

By train. In addition to Amtrak routes, commuter rail transportation is provided in eastern Massachusetts and between Boston and Providence by the Massachusetts Bay Transportation Authority (tel: 617-222-3200/1-800-392-6100; www.mbta.com). The MBTA also operates Boston's system of subways (called 'the T'), trolleys, and elevated trains.

To use the subway, purchase a Charlie Ticket ($2) from the machines in the stations. A single ticket permits travel on the entire 'Outbound' length of a line, but there's an 'Inbound' surcharge on extensions of the Green Line. If you board the T at surface stations where there is no ticket machine, you will need the exact fare as conductors do not carry change. The Charlie Card is a plastic stored-value card. If you use this, then each ride is $1.70 and you can get free transfers to MBTA buses (not possible with the Charlie Tickets). Accompanied children under 11 travel free.

By bus. An MBTA bus service connects Boston with its suburbs and outlying cities. Other city areas in New England also have a local bus service. For inter-city bus travel within the region, contact Greyhound *(see opposite)* or Peter Pan Bus Lines (tel: 1-800-343-9999; www.peterpanbus.com). Plymouth and Brockton Buses (tel: 508-746-0378; www.p-b.com) link Boston with Cape Cod and Massachusetts's South Shore, while C&J (tel: 603-430-1100; www.ridecj.com) offers a bus service between Boston and Portsmouth.

By ferry. Between May and mid-October it is possible to catch ferries from Boston to Salem (www.salemferry.com) and to Provincetown (www.bostonharborcruises.com and www.baystatecruisecompany.com).

VISAS AND PASSPORTS

To enter the US you must have a passport valid for at least six months longer than your intended stay. Visas are required for some nationalities, and also for stays exceeding prescribed time limits. A few countries (including the UK) are part of the Visa Waiver Program allowing citizens to enter the country for 90 days or less without obtaining a visa. Consult the nearest US embassy or consulate in your home country or check www.travel.state.gov.

Above from far left: fall in Vermont; Boston ferries.

Taxis
• Portland, Maine: ASAP Taxi, tel: 207-791-2727, www.asaptaxi.net.
• Boston, Massachusetts: Boston Cab, tel: 617-536-5010; Checker Cab, tel: 617-536-7000; Town Taxi, tel: 617-536-5000.
• Cambridge, Massachusetts: Cambridge Checker Cab, tel: 617-497-1500; Yellow Cab, tel: 617-876-5000.
• Portsmouth, New Hampshire: Blue Star Taxi, tel: 603-436-2774, www.bluestartaxi.com.
• Providence, Rhode Island: Airport Taxis, tel: 401-737-2868, www.airporttaxiri.com.
• Burlington, Vermont: New England Taxis, tel: 802-598-7254, www.newenglandtaxi.com.

You will seldom be far from a hotel, motel, inn, or B&B in New England, so making up a route as you go is quite feasible. However, if you want to stay at a particular place, advance reservations are recommended and are particularly important any time in summer, in the fall 'leaf-peeping' season, and near popular winter resort areas. During these times, some accommodations raise their rates and have a two-night minimum-stay policy over the weekend.

Boston (MA)

Boston Harbor Hotel

70 Rowes Wharf; tel: 617-439-7000; www.bhh.com; T-stop: Aquarium; $$$$

Board the airport water shuttle at Logan and, seven minutes later, step into one of the city's premier waterside hotels. Each of the 230 rooms has either a harbor or a skyline view. Eighteen rooms are designed for the physically disabled. Museum-quality art decorates the public areas, and the Meritage restaurant offers superb dining.

The Langham

250 Franklin Street; tel: 617-451-1900; http://boston.langhamhotels.com; T-stop: State; $$$$

This luxurious hotel, occupying the former Federal Reserve Bank, has rooms decorated to reflect the building's opulent history. Its Café Fleuri offers a brasserie-style menu and an elaborate Sunday jazz brunch.

Liberty Hotel

215 Charles Street; tel: 617-224-4000; www.libertyhotel.com; T-stop: Charles/MGH; $$$$

The former Charles Street Jail (built in 1851) has been inventively renovated into this boutique hotel. Original prison catwalks and magnificent soaring windows have been preserved. The prison theme continues in the restaurant Clink and stylish bar Alibi. Also here is the contemporary Italian restaurant Scampo run by celebrity chef Lydia Shire.

Newbury Guest House

261 Newbury Street; tel: 617-670-6000/1-800-437-7668; www.newburyguesthouse.com; T-stop: Hynes; $$

Three 1880s Victorian homes have been renovated to create this elegant 32-room inn. The rooms retain some of the 19th-century decorative details. There are quieter rooms in the back.

Nine Zero

90 Tremont Street; tel: 617-772-5800; www.ninezero.com; T-stop: Park Street; $$$$

One of Boston's sleekest boutique hotels, offering high-tech, high-speed,

Price for a double room for one night without breakfast:	
$$$$	over $200
$$$	$150–200
$$	$75–150
$	under $75

and high-touch amenities, along with personalized service, custom-designed beds, and down comforters. The restaurant, KO Prime, serves superb steaks.

Ritz-Carlton, Boston Common

2 Avery Street; tel: 617-574-7100/ 1-800-241-3333; www.ritzcarlton. com; T-stop: Boylston; $$$$

Overlooking the Common, the modern Ritz-Carlton offers contemporary luxury minus the stuffiness that hung over its former property (now the Taj Boston) across from the Public Garden. All the rooms have modern furnishings. High tea is served in the Galleria.

Cambridge (MA)

Charles Hotel

1 Bennett Street; tel: 617-864-1200; www.charleshotel.com; T-stop: Harvard; $$$$

The Charles Hotel offers restrained Shaker-inspired luxury, with incredible antique quilts gracing the walls, and impeccable service. All 294 rooms are well appointed and include high-tech amenities. The Regatta Bar is a great jazz venue, and the Rialto restaurant is a mainstay of the city's gourmet circuit.

The Inn at Harvard

1201 Massachusetts Avenue; tel: 617-491-2222/1-800-458-5886; www.innatharvard.com; T-stop: Harvard; $$

Architect and Harvard graduate Graham Gund designed this four-story hotel to blend in with the university. The 111 rooms, built around an atrium, are delightful and were all renovated in 2006.

Mary Prentiss Inn

6 Prentiss Street; tel: 617-661-2929; www.maryprentissinn.com; T-stop: Porter; $$$

This historic Greek Revival building has 20 rooms with exposed beams, shutters, and antiques; some have wood-burning fireplaces and Jacuzzis. Rates include a full breakfast and complimentary afternoon tea. There is a lush outdoor deck, and free parking.

Concord (MA)

Hawthorne Inn

462 Lexington Road; tel: 978-369-5610; www.concordmass.com; $$

Apart from the town's Colonial Inn *(see p.47)*, another highly recommended overnight stay is this 1870s house opposite The Wayside, which sports delightfully decorated rooms.

Salem and Cape Ann (MA)

The Addison Choate Inn

49 Broadway, Rockport; tel: 1-800-245-7543; www.addisonchoateinn. com; $$

A charming 1850s house that offers modern conveniences such as wifi. It has six rooms, and there is a separate cottage with two self-catering units.

Above from far left: balcony view from the Boston Harbor Hotel; The Langham's historic Federal Reserve Bank facade.

Free Calls
Toll-free numbers starting 1-888 or 1-800 are valid in the US for out-of-state calls.

Hostels
Hosteling International New England (tel: 617-718-7990; www.hinewengland.org) has one year-round and one summer hostel in Boston and four in Cape Cod. There are also hostels in Maine and Vermont run by Hosteling International USA (tel: 301-495-1240; www.hiusa.org).

Hawthorne Hotel

18 Washington Square West, Salem; tel: 978-744-4080; www.hawthornehotel.com; $$–$$$

This Federal-style red-brick building is situated by the common and handy for all downtown attractions. The rooms are all furnished with 18th-century reproductions. Facilities include a restaurant, bar, lounge, and exercise room.

Yankee Clipper Inn

96 Granite Street, Rockport; tel: 978-546-3407; www.yankeeclipperinn.com; $$$–$$$$

This 1929 Art Deco oceanfront mansion has well-appointed and charmingly decorated guest rooms (six look out to sea) and a saltwater pool.

South Shore and Cape Cod (MA)

The Brass Key

67 Bradford Street, Provincetown; tel: 1800-842-9858; www.brasskey.com; $$$

A stylish guesthouse complex made up of four converted houses surrounding a small pool. There is also a spa, and all rooms have air-conditioning and wifi.

The Dan'l Webster Inn

149 Main Street, Sandwich; tel: 508-888-3622/1-800-444-3566; www.danlwebsterinn.com; $$$$

Lodgings have been available here for guests for the last 300 years. It is named after the successful Boston lawyer and US senator. There are 48 rooms and suites, gardens, a spa, and an outdoor heated swimming pool.

Provincetown Inn

1 Commerical Street, Provincetown; tel: 508-487-9500; www.provincetowninn.com; $$

A motel-style resort bounded by water on three sides, with its own pool and direct access to the beach. Good value for Provincetown.

Whitfield House

26 North Street, Plymouth; tel: 508-747-6735; www.whitfieldhouse.com; $$

This charming B&B, in a house dating from 1782, offers fireplaces, antique furniture, and canopy beds in three of its four bedrooms.

The Berkshires and Pioneer Valley (MA)

Deerfield Inn

81 Main Street, Deerfield; tel: 413-774-5587/1-800-926-3865; www.deerfieldinn.com; $$$

All of the rooms at this 1884 inn have period wallpaper and furnishings; some

Price for a double room for one night without breakfast:	
$$$$	over $200
$$$	$150–200
$$	$75–150
$	under $75

have four-poster or canopy beds. The common rooms are filled with antiques, and there's also Champney's restaurant, featuring a contemporary American menu and 101 different Martinis.

The Porches Inn

231 River Street, North Adams; tel: 413-664-0400; www.porches. com; $$$

This stylish inn across the road from MASS MoCA offers 47 imaginatively decorated rooms that pay quirky homage to the town's former mill workers. There's a pool and wifi.

The Red Lion Inn

30 Main Street, Stockbridge; tel: 413-298-1690; www.redlioninn. com; $$–$$$$

It hardly gets more traditional than this historic 108-room inn, dating back to 1773 and immortalized in Norman Rockwell's painting *Main Street, Stockbridge*. Six presidents have stayed here as well as John Wayne and Bob Dylan. Sit on the front porch and watch the world go by, or dine in its elegant restaurant hung with chandeliers.

Providence (RI)

Hotel Providence

311 Westminster Street; tel: 401-861-8000/1-800-861-8990; www.thehotelprovidence.com; $$$

On trendified Westminster Street is this boutique 80-room property, which has benefited from the design skills of a Rhode Island School of Design professor. Its sophisticated Aspire restaurant gets the thumbs up from locals for a fancy meal.

Providence Biltmore

11 Dorrance Street; tel: 401-421-0700; www.providencebiltmore.com; $$–$$$

Old World elegance at the heart of downtown Providence has been the Biltmore's stock in trade for decades. Recent renovations have restored the grande dame's glamour.

Newport (RI)

The Ivy Lodge

12 Clay Street; tel: 401-849-6865/ 1-800-834-6865; www.ivylodge. com; $$–$$$

This Victorian 'cottage' in the mansion district features a 33ft (10m) high Gothic paneled oak entrance and a three-story turned-baluster stairway. Guest rooms have private baths, period furnishings, brass or iron beds, and fireplaces. Hearty buffet-style breakfasts.

The Hotel Viking

1 Bellevue Avenue; tel: 401-847-3300/1-800-556-7126; www.hotelviking.com; $$$–$$$$

This property on the National Register of Historic Places blends bygone detail with guest comforts. Rooms – particularly suites – are spacious and well equipped. There's a pool, hot tub, sauna, restaurant, and rooftop bar.

Above from far left: Boston skyline view from the Liberty Hotel *(also pictured on pp.94–5)*; The Brass Key.

B&Bs
For listings of B&Bs and guesthouses in New England, check Inns and Resorts of New England (www.innsandresortsofnewengland.com).
Other useful websites for Boston and Massachusetts include www.boston-bnbagency.com, www.hosthomesofboston.com, www.bbreserve.com, and www.bnbboston.com.
Helpful general websites include www.visitnewengland.com, www.discovernewengland.org, and www.bnbfinder.com.

Griswold Inn

36 Main Street, Essex; tel: 860-767-1776; www.griswoldinn.com; $$–$$$
Dating back to 1776, this is one of the oldest inns in the US. All rooms have private baths and period furnishings, and some have fireplaces. There is an atmospheric taproom (bar), and a restaurant that serves classic New England fare; Sunday brunch is a tradition.

Steamboat Inn

73 Steamboat Wharf, Mystic; tel: 860-536-8300; www.steamboatinnmystic.com; $$$–$$$$
This renovated riverfront warehouse is a good choice for luxurious accommodations. Big rooms have been beautifully decorated and have whirlpool baths; some of them feature wet bars and fireplaces.

Study at Yale

1157 Chapel Street, New Haven; tel: 203-503-3900; www.studyhotels.com; $$$–$$$$
A lovely, designer boutique hotel, steps away from the heart of the campus. Spacious rooms are decorated in calming colors and a tasteful mix of contemporary and traditional furnishing, including leather reading chairs.

Whalers' Inn

20 East Main Street, Mystic; tel: 860-536-1506/1-800-243-2588; www.whalersinnmystic.com; $$–$$$
Located one block from the Mystic River, this complex includes a small hotel with Victorian furnishings and reproduction four-poster beds, and the fancy Italian restaurant Bravo Bravo.

The Inn at Weston

630 Main Street, Weston; tel: 802-824-6789; www.innweston.com; $$–$$$$
The original inn at this three-building complex dates from 1848. Accommodations are luxurious, with fresh-cut flowers, wood-burning fireplaces, and whirlpool tubs for two. Contemporary regional cuisine is served in the candle-lit dining room.

The Latchis

50 Main Street, Brattleboro; tel: 802-254-6300; www.latchis.com; $$
Occupying part of a handsome 1938 Art Deco building, which also includes a beautifully preserved cinema of the era, is this great-value hotel run under the stewardship of the Brattleboro Arts Initiative – hence the work by local artists displayed in each room.

> **Price for a double room for one night without breakfast:**
>
> | | |
> |---|---|
> | $$$$ | over $200 |
> | $$$ | $150–200 |
> | $$ | $75–150 |
> | $ | under $75 |

Woodstock Inn and Resort

14 The Green, Woodstock;
tel: 802-457-1100/1-800-448-7900;
www.woodstockinn.com; $$$–$$$$
An elegant, historic inn, where the spacious guest rooms have colonial furnishings and some have porches and/or fireplaces. Amenities include a fine restaurant, tavern, swimming pool, and nearby golf course.

Burlington and Lake Champlain Valley (VT)

Basin Harbor Club

Basin Harbor Road, Vergennes;
tel: 802-475-2311/1-800-622-4000;
www.basinharbor.com; $$$–$$$$
This gracious lakefront resort, situated on 700 acres (283ha), has fine views across Lake Champlain and offers comfortable accommodations in cottages or in rooms and suites in lodges. Activities on offer include an 18-hole golf course, boating on the lake, children's programs, and tennis. The restaurant serves classic American cuisine; jackets and ties are required at dinner. Closed mid-Oct–mid-May.

The Chipman Inn

Route 125, Ripton; tel: 802-388-
2390; www.chipmaninn.com; $–$$
In a tranquil spot within the Green Mountains National Forest, and close by the nature walk to poet Robert Frost's cabin, is this charming, simple inn with a private bar and spacious, country-style rooms.

Inn at Shelburne Farms

Bay and Harbor Road, Shelburne;
tel: 802-985-8498; www.shelburne
farms.org; $$$–$$$$
The grand 1899 Webb family mansion, on the grounds of a working farm and National Historic Landmark, offers 24 luxurious, period-decorated guest rooms, an excellent library, spectacular views of Lake Champlain, and some of Vermont's finest dining. Closed mid-Oct–mid-May.

The Middlebury Inn

14 Court Square, Middlebury;
tel: 802-388-4961/1-800-842-4666;
www.middleburyinn.com; $$–$$$$
A rambling and creaking brick inn from 1827, with well restored and appointed rooms in the main inn and the Victorian-era Porter House Mansion, as well as accommodations in the attached contemporary motel. Afternoon tea, included in the rates, is served daily 2.30–5.30pm.

The Lakes Region (NH)

The Wolfeboro Inn

90 North Main Street, Wolfeboro;
tel: 603-451-2389; www.wolfeboro
inn.com; $$$–$$$$
There are lake views from the balconies of some of the recently renovated rooms at this attractive property with a private beach beside the water. Its Wolfe's Tavern, hung with pewter mugs, is a convivial place for a relaxed meal or drink.

Above from far left: aerial view of the Basin Harbor Club and a lakeside dining terrace at the resort; The Middlebury Inn.

The White Mountains (NH)

Adair Country Inn
80 Guider Lane, Bethlehem; tel: 603-444-2600; www.adairinn.com; $$$

This luxurious Georgian Revival mansion, set in 200 acres (80ha) overlooking the Presidential Mountain range, offers nine antiques-decorated guest rooms. The restaurant (Thur–Mon) is open to outside guests for dinner.

Adventure Suites
3440 White Mountain Highway, North Conway; tel: 603-356-9744; www.adventuresuites.com; $–$$$

Your kids (and the child inside you) will be in raptures if you check into this whacky theme hotel. All rooms are different and they include ones designed as a tree house, a log cabin, and a cave with stalactites and a waterfall shower.

AMC Highland Center
Route 302, Crawfold Notch; tel: 603-278-4453; www.outdoors.org; $

Ideal for hikers, this place offers simple shared and private accommodations and an environmental learning center. Meals are available from a self-serve canteen.

AMC Pinkham Notch Camp and Huts
Route 16, Pinkham Notch (reservations: Box 298, Gorham); tel: 603-466-2727; www.outdoors.org; $

These accommodations at the base of Mount Washington include bunk, private, and family rooms, all with shared bath. Three meals are served daily, and there's a living room with a fireplace.

Mount Washington Hotel and Resort
Route 302, Bretton Woods; tel: 603-278-1000/1-800-258-0330; www.mtwashington.com; $$$$

This grande dame of the White Mountains opened in 1902 and is still going strong. It offers a wide variety of accommodations, plus activities including golf, skiing, and a state-of-the-art spa. Men should bring a jacket and tie to dine in the formal dining room in the evening. A lovely, quieter place to stay is the resort's elegant Bretton Arms Inn.

Portsmouth (NH)

Ale House Inn
121 Bow Street; tel: 603-431-7760; www.alehouseinn.com; $$–$$$$

This recently renovated hotel occupies the second floor of an old brick brewery (hence the name). Some of the contemporary design rooms provide glimpses of the river. No food is served, but there are plenty of places to eat nearby.

Sise Inn
40 Court Street; tel: 603-433-1200; www.siseinn.com; $$–$$$$

Set in a Queen Anne townhouse (and modern addition) in the city's most historic district. Rooms are decorated with antique reproductions and have private baths; some have whirlpool baths.

Portland and Midcoast Maine

Camden Harbour Inn

83 Bayview Street, Camden; tel: 207-236-4200/1-800-236-4266; www.camdenharbourinn.com; $$$$

Enjoy lovely views, king-size feather beds, and contemporary boutique furnishings in dramatic colors at this super-stylish hotel. Also drop by for its award-winning restaurant, Natalie's (www.nataliesrestaurant.com; daily 5.30–9pm).

Camden Maine Stay

22 High Street, Camden; tel: 207-236-9636; www.camdenmaine stay.com; $$–$$$$

This 200-year-old colonial inn has eight comfortable, air-conditioned, eclectically decorated rooms, and two parlors with wood-burning fireplaces. Full breakfast can be taken on the porch overlooking the garden.

Morrill Mansion Bed and Breakfast

249 Vaughan Street, Portland; tel: 207-774-6900/1-888-5667-7455; www.morrillmansion.com; $$–$$$

This charming 19th-century townhouse in Portland's historic West End has been beautifully restored. The seven rooms benefit from modern amenities, such as cable TV, spa tubs, and wifi.

Portland Harbor Hotel

468 Fore Street, Portland; tel: 207-775-9090/1-888-798-9090; www.portlandharborhotel.com; $$$$

In the heart of the city's Old Port District, this fine hotel offers bags of character and all the amenities you could need. Some rooms open out directly onto the lovely courtyard garden.

Down East Maine

The Bass Cottage Inn

14 The Field, Bar Harbor; tel: 207-288-1234; www.basscottage.com; $$$$

A baby grand piano in the spacious lounge sets the tone at this gracious guesthouse, which holds back on the heritage decor that features prominently in many other Bar Harbor abodes.

The Castine Inn

Main Street, PO Box 41, Castine; tel: 207-326-4365; www.castineinn.com; $–$$

Opened in 1898 and located near the harbor, the gracious Castine Inn offers spacious accommodations. Guests can enjoy the sauna, a wraparound porch, and a common room with a fireplace. The award-winning chef/owner also conducts cooking classes here.

Price for a double room for one night without breakfast:	
$$$$	over $200
$$$	$150–200
$$	$75–150
$	under $75

RESTAURANTS

Wood-paneled and beamed colonial dining rooms, retro-styled diners, sophisticated flights of culinary fancy, and seafood enjoyed within sight of the harbors where it was landed – all these experiences and more are available in the region's eclectic spread of restaurants and cafés.

Boston (MA)

Bricco Enoteca & Lounge

241 Hanover Street, North End; tel: 617-248-6800; www.bricco. com; Mon–Fri 5pm–2am, Sat–Sun noon–4pm, 5pm–2am; $$$$

This upscale boutique Italian restaurant prepares regional treats including handmade pasta. The waiters will urge you to order a 'traditional' meal with several courses, so come prepared with an empty stomach and full wallet.

The Daily Catch

323 Hanover Street, North End; tel: 617-523-8567; www.daily catch.com; daily 11am–10pm, Fri–Sat until 11pm; $$

This tiny hole-in-the-wall institution specializes in Sicilian seafood.

Price for a three-course dinner for one, excluding beverages, tax, and tip:

$$$$	over $60
$$$	$40–60
$$	$20–40
$	below $20

Figs

67 Main Street, Charlestown; tel: 617-242-2229; Mon–Thur 5.30–10pm, Fri–Sat until 10.30pm, Sun 4.30–9pm; $$

Celebrity chef Todd English's gourmet pizzeria serves excellent thin-crust pizza, grilled in wood-fired ovens and topped with a variety of epicurean toppings. The fig and prosciutto special is a favorite. There's a second location at 24 Charles Street, Beacon Hill (tel: 617-742-3447).

Ivy

49 Temple Place, Downtown; tel: 617-451-1416; www.ivyrestaurant group.com; Mon–Thur 11am–3pm, 5–11pm, Fri 11am–midnight, Sat 4pm–midnight, Sun 4–11pm; $$–$$$

A stylish modern restaurant and bar that serves simple lunches and small sharing plates for dinner. Really buzzes after work when young professionals stop in for a drink.

KO Prime

Nine Zero Hotel, 90 Tremont Street, Downtown; tel: 617-772-0202; www.koprimeboston.com; Mon–Fri 6.30–10.30am, 11.30am–2pm, 5.30–10pm, Sat 8am–2pm, 5.30–10pm, Sun 8am–2pm, 5.30–9.30pm; $$$

Chef Ken Oringer's stylish steakhouse, decorated with cow hide, emphasizes farm-fresh produce, including grass-fed Kobe and Wagyu beef, and seafood. The wine list is extensive and well chosen.

Locke-Ober

3 Winter Place, Downtown; tel: 617-542-1340; www.lockeober.com; Mon–Thur 11.30am–2.30pm, 5.30–10pm, Fri until 11pm, Sat 5.30–11pm; $$$

Celebrity chef Lydia Shire created a stir when she took over this handsome dining room, which had previously banned women for 97 years. Many traditional favorites, such as JFK's lobster stew and calf's liver with bacon, are still available, spruced up with Shire's contemporary touches. Denim and sneakers are only allowed in the bar area.

Olives

10 City Square, Charlestown; tel: 617-242-1999; www.toddenglish. com; Mon–Fri 5.30–10pm, Sat 5–10.30pm, Sun 5–9pm; $$$$

The original restaurant that put chef Todd English on the culinary map. The Italian cuisine is creative, and a wood-fired oven is used to excellent effect to cook meats and other dishes served with signature sauces like pistachio pesto.

Cambridge (MA)

Café Algiers

40 Brattle Street; tel: 617-492-1557; daily 8.30am–10.45pm; $$

Hang out with Harvard's boho crowd at this atmospheric, North African-styled place, serving a reasonably priced menu of well prepared Middle Eastern standards. The falafel has a unique twist and the handmade lamb sausage is seasoned to perfection.

Casablanca

40 Brattle Street; tel: 617-876-0999; Mon–Thur 11.30am–2.30pm, 5.30–10pm, Fri–Sat until 10.30pm, Sun 11am–3pm, 5.30–10pm; $$–$$$

In the same complex as Café Algiers, this buzzing and reliable place takes its design cues from the famous Bogart movie. It offers a Mediterranean menu with refreshing interpretations of Middle Eastern dishes, with tapas available at the bar tables.

Harvest

44 Brattle Street; tel: 617-868-2255; www.harvestcambridge.com; Mon–Thur and Sun noon–2.30pm, 5.30–10pm, Fri–Sat until 11pm; $$$

As the name suggests, chef Mary Dumont focuses on the region's freshest seasonal ingredients to prepare dishes interpreted from around the world. The atmosphere is relaxed, but has a distinct business account feel. It offers dining in one of the few garden terraces around Harvard Square.

Rialto

Charles Hotel, 1 Bennett Street; tel: 617-661-5050; www.rialto-restaurant. com; Mon–Fri 5.30–10pm, Sat 5.30–11pm, Sun 5.30–9pm; $$$$

Perennial favorite of gourmands is this restaurant specializing in regional Italian cuisine and seafood. Menu changes region and ingredients seasonally. The wine list offers an interesting range from organic and small vineyards.

Above from far left: open kitchen and dining room at Olives; Rialto serves top Italian cuisine.

Reservations
Generally, there is no need to sweat about scoring a table at even the hottest chef's table. Nevertheless, you would be well advised to make an advance booking for Friday or Saturday nights; try the online booking service www.open table.com. Note also that some places don't take reservations at all, so either turn up early or be prepared to wait.

Franklin Cape Ann

118 Main Street, Gloucester; tel: 978-283-7888; www.franklincafe. com; daily 4.30pm–1am; $$–$$$

Dine on dishes such as lobster BLT and homemade gnocchi at this sophisticated restaurant and bar that's the North Shore outpost of the original in Boston's trendy South End.

The Lyceum

43 Church Street, Salem; tel: 978-745-7665; Mon–Fri and Sun 11.30am–2.30pm, daily 5.30–10pm; $$$

Contemporary American cuisine is served in the elegant surroundings of the building where Alexander Graham Bell made the first long-distance telephone call.

Ross's Grill

Whaler's Wharf, 237 Commercial Street, Provincetown; tel: 508-487-8878; www.rossgrillptown.com; Thur–Mon 11.30am–3.30pm, 5.30–10pm; $$$

> Price for a three-course dinner for one, excluding beverages, tax, and tip:
>
> $$$$ over $60
> $$$ $40–60
> $$ $20–40
> $ below $20

Intimate and friendly Ross's is the epitome of relaxed fine dining, with excellent bistro-style dishes such as steak frites and crispy Tuscan cod. Offers a wide selection of wines by the glass.

Sal's Place

99 Commercial Street, Provincetown; tel: 508-487-1279; www. salsplaceofprovincetown.com; May–Oct daily 5.30–10pm; $$

When other places are booked up, it is often possible to squeeze in at Sal's, an authentic Italian joint in the West End with a romantic beachside terrace. The portions are huge and always come with a side order of pasta.

Allium

42–44 Railroad Street, Great Barrington; tel: 413-528-2118; www. mezzeinc.com/allium; Sun–Thur 5–9.30pm, Fri–Sat 5–10pm; $$–$$$

The best of local ingredients are used for the appealing modern American dishes served at this relaxed restaurant, a star-pick among local foodies.

Bizen

17 Railroad Street, Great Barrington; tel: 413-528-4343; daily noon–2.30pm, 5–9.30pm; $$$–$$$$

A fine Japanese restaurant in the Berkshires? You'd better believe it – customers and critics rave about the quality of the

sushi and other traditional dishes with quirky Americanized names.

Truc Orient Express

3 Harris Street, West Stockbridge; tel: 413-232-4204; daily 11am–10pm; $$

Creative dishes, such as 'Happy Pancake' and 'Shaking Beef', are elegantly presented in this upscale Vietnamese restaurant.

Providence (RI)

Blue Grotto Restaurant

210 Atwells Avenue; tel: 401-272-9030; www.bluegrottorestaurant.com; Mon–Fri 11.30am–2pm, 5–10pm, Fri until 10.30pm, Sat 11.30am–3pm, 4.30–10.30pm, Sun noon–9pm; $$–$$$

Excellent fried calamari, spinach ravioli, or *bistecca fiorentina* is dished up at this mainstay of the Federal Hill Italian neighborhood.

Bravo

123 Empire Street; tel: 401-490-5112; www.bravobrasserie.com; Sun–Thur 11am–1am, Fri–Sat until 2am; $$$

Freshly baked baguettes set the tone at this American bistro inspired by French-style cafés.

Newport (RI)

Salvation Café

140 Broadway; tel: 401-847-2620; www.salvationcafe.com; café daily 5–10pm, Fri–Sat until 11pm; $$

With a fun menu and decor that hop around the world for inspiration, and reasonable prices for upmarket Newport, this is a cool place to hang out. The bar serves drinks until midnight.

The Spiced Pear

The Chanler at Cliff Walk, 117 Memorial Boulevard; tel: 401-847-2244; www.spicedpear.com: $$$$

If you are going to push the boat out, do it in style with the delicious gourmand tasting menu at this super-elegant restaurant, part of a luxurious boutique hotel. In good weather dine on the verandah with ocean views.

Connecticut Coast

Café Routier

1353 Boston Post Road, Old Saybrook; tel: 860-399-8700; www.cafe routier.com; daily 5–9pm; $$$

Artfully prepared French and American dishes, a fine wine list, and candlelit tables with white linen tablecloths all contribute to this restaurant's classy reputation.

Ibiza

39 High Street, New Haven; tel: 203-865-1933; www.ibizanewhaven.com; Mon–Thur 5–9pm, Fri noon–2.30pm, 5–10pm, Sat 5–10pm; $$$$

Traditional and modern Spanish cuisine shines in this restaurant, which is based in what was once a car park designed by local-architect-made-good César Pelli.

Burlington and Lake Champlain Valley (VT)

Bearded Frog

5247 Shelburne Road, Shelburne; tel: 802-985-9877; www.thebearded frog.com; daily 5–9pm; $$$

Located in a restored 19th-century farmhouse, this gastropub serves dishes as diverse as crunchy tofu cakes and buttermilk-marinated pork chops.

Leunig's Bistro

115 Church Street, Burlington; tel: 802-863-3759; www.leunigs bistro.com; Mon–Thur 11am–10pm, Fri 11am–11pm, Sat 9am–11pm, Sun 9am–10pm; $$

Art Nouveau rules at this atmospheric French bistro with a fine menu.

The Green Mountains (VT)

Simon Pearce Restaurant

1760 Quechee Main Street, Quechee; tel: 802-295-1470; www.simonpearce.com; daily 11.30am–9pm; $$$$

A short drive out of Woodstock is this lovely restaurant in an old mill overlooking the Ottauquechee River. Fine country cuisine is prepared using local produce.

T.J. Buckley's

132 Elliot Street, Brattleboro; tel: 802-257-4922; Wed–Sun 6–9pm; $$$

Typical of this quirky town is this eight-table restaurant serving top-flight cuisine out of a snug little 1927 diner.

The Lakes Region (NH)

Shibley's Drive-In

On the Pier, Alton Bay; tel: 603-875-3636; daily Nov–Apr 11am–5pm, May–Oct 11am–10pm; $

Pause at this humble pitstop for 24 flavors of soft-serve ice cream, plus burgers or sandwiches, which you can take across the road to enjoy beside the lake.

The White Mountains (NH)

The 1785 Inn

Route 16, Intervale; tel: 603-356-9025; www.the1785inn.com; daily 5–9pm; $$$

With a huge fireplace and a colonial atmosphere, this inn has an extensive list of appetizers, creative continental entrées, and a superb wine list.

Portsmouth (NH)

The Dunway Restaurant at Strawbery Banke

66 Marcy Street; tel: 603-373-6112; www.dunawayrestaurant.com; Tue–Sat 5.30am–9.30pm, Fri–Sat 11.30am–2.30pm; $$$$

The award-winning contemporary American cuisine and charming historic atmosphere make this a memorable place to round off a day in Portsmouth.

The Library Restaurant

401 State Street; tel: 603-431-5202; www.libraryrestaurant.com; daily 11.30am–3pm, 5–9.30pm; $$–$$$

A wood-paneled steakhouse in elegant Rockingham House, built in 1785.

Portland and Midcoast Maine

Bresca

111 Middle Street, Portland; tel: 207-772-1004; www.bresca.org; Tue–Sat 5.30–9.30pm; $$$

Book ahead for one of the 20 seats at this tiny Italian-American charmer, with dishes such as sea urchin linguine and honey-glazed duck breast.

Five Fifty-Five

555 Congress Street, Portland; tel: 207-761-0555; www.fivefifty-five.com; daily 5–9.30pm, Fri–Sat until 10.30pm, Sun 9.30am–2pm; $$$–$$$$

The truffled lobster 'mac and cheese' is decadent, and don't miss out on delicious modern remakes of old classics, such as 'not your grandmother's roast chicken' and the 'beets me' salad.

Fore Street

288 Fore Street, Portland; tel: 207-775-2217; www.forestreet.biz; daily 5.30–10pm, Fri–Sat until 10.30pm; $$$–$$$$

One of the many successful restaurants that have refocused attention on Portland's Old Port District. A changing daily menu reflects all the great produce that's available in this city, with an emphasis on grilled meats and fish.

Primo

25 Main Street, Rockland; tel: 207-596-0770; www.primorestaurant. com; Apr–Oct Wed–Sun 5.30–9pm, July–Aug also Mon; $$$$

Featuring seasonal produce from its own gardens, this top-class restaurant is based inside a Victorian home and has transformed Rockland into a foodie destination.

Down East Maine

Café This Way

14½ Mount Desert Street, Bar Harbor; tel: 207-288-4483; http://cafethisway. com; May–Oct Mon–Sat 7–11am, Sun 8am–1pm, daily 5.30–9pm; $$–$$$

If you don't make it to this local favorite for breakfast, you get a second chance at dinner to sample the fun atmosphere and menu, featuring dishes such as smoked duck-wrapped scallops.

Pentagöet Inn

26 Main Street, Castine; tel: 207-326-8616; www.pentagoet.com; daily 6–9.30pm; $$$–$$$$

This Victorian inn not only has charming rooms but also a top-class kitchen turning out delicious meals using local produce. The cosy Passports Pub is hung with vintage photos and paintings.

Price for a three-course dinner for one, excluding beverages, tax, and tip:

$$$$	over $60
$$$	$40–60
$$	$20–40
$	below $20

Boston (MA)

Berklee College of Music

1140 Boylston Street; tel: 617-266-1400; www.berklee.edu

Founded in 1945, this is the world's largest independent music college with a highly regarded jazz program attracting students from around the globe. Faculty, student, and recording artists regularly perform in the college's many venues.

Boston Symphony Hall

301 Massachusetts Avenue; tel: 617-266-1200; www.bso.org

The acoustically impeccable 1900 building is home to the renowned Boston Symphony Orchestra and, in summer (when the BSO performs at Tanglewood in Lenox) and during the Christmas holidays, its less formal off-shoot, the Boston Pops Orchestra. Tickets can be hard to come by.

Citi Performing Arts Center

270 Tremont Street; tel: 866-348-9738; www.citicenter.org/theatres

Comprising both the historic Wang and Shubert theaters, this is a focus for the major performing arts in Boston.

Club Café

209 Columbus Avenue; tel: 617-536-0966; www.clubcafe.com

A popular gay complex and the place to be on Thursday nights, with a quieter bar and restaurant at the front and thumping music videos in the back.

Colonial Theatre

106 Boylston Street; tel: 617-426-9366; www.bostonscolonialtheatre.com

An ornate venue, featuring big names and popular shows.

Felt

533 Washington Street; tel: 617-350-5555; www.feltclubboston.com

Local celebs, such as Ben Affleck and Matt Damon, drop by this happening spot, combining bar, billiard hall, restaurant, and DJs on Fridays and Saturdays. There's a dress code.

Good Life

28 Kingston Street; tel: 617-451-2622; www.goodlifebar.com

A popular after-work bar with an impressive vodka menu and inventive nibbles. Walls act as a regularly changing gallery of art and DJs energize the often packed dance floor.

Goody Glover's

50 Salem Street; tel: 617-367-6444; www.goodyglovers.com

A neighborhood landmark known for its traditional Irish grub and laid-back vibe.

Jacob Wirth

31 Stuart Street; tel: 617-338-8586; www.jacobwirth.com

This time-warp pub and restaurant in the Theater District, established in 1868, serves an impressive list of beers.

Jordan Hall, New England Conservatory

30 Gainsborough Street; tel: 617-585-1260; http://necmusic.edu

This music school hosts the Boston Philharmonic as well as guest orchestras and chamber music concerts.

Paradise Rock Club

967–969 Commonwealth Avenue; tel: 617-562-8800; www.thedise.com

Boston's top venue for established and up-and-coming rock and alternative pop music.

Wilbur Theatre

246 Tremont Street; tel: 617-931-2000; www.thewilburtheatre.com

This 1914 theater is currently home to the long-running Comedy Connection, showcasing top comedians and singers.

Cambridge (MA)

Club Passim

47 Palmer Street; tel: 617-492-7679; www.clubpassim.org;

The US's oldest folk club hosts a variety of local and national artists, focusing on folk, world, and bluegrass music.

Grendel's Den

89 Winthrop Street; tel: 617-491-1160; www.grendelsden.com

An unpretentious student hangout.

Loeb Drama Center

64 Brattle Street; tel: 617-547-8300; www.amrep.org

Home of the American Repertory Theater, which presents classic and first-run drama.

Regatta Bar

Charles Hotel, 1 Bennett Street; tel: 617-661-5000; www.regattabarjazz.com

A fashionable bar on the third floor of the Charles Hotel, featuring top jazz and R&B acts in a sophisticated interior. Bookings recommended.

T.T. the Bear's Place

10 Brookline Street; tel: 617-492-0082; www.ttthebears.com

One of the best places in greater Boston to catch live music any night of the week, in a relaxed and friendly atmosphere. Last-minute tickets can be bought at the door with cash only.

South Shore and Cape Cod (MA)

Atlantic House

6 Masonic Place, Provincetown; tel: 508-487-3821; www.ahouse.com

The playwright Eugene O'Neil once drank here. It's now a popular gay complex of a couple of bars and dance club with a variety of theme nights.

Cape Cod Melody Tent

21 West Main Street, Hyannis; tel: 508-775-9100; www.melodytent.org

This tent theater presents a mixture of top musical and comedy acts from across the spectrum.

Above from far left: Grendel's Den, a Harvard hangout; the bar at Felt.

Opening Hours
Pubs and lounges typically open daily around 4 or 5pm. In Boston, by law, they all have to stop serving alcohol at 2am (1am Sun–Wed in Cambridge). Elsewhere in New England bar opening hours may be longer.

Comedy Scene

Among the top US comedians to have kick-started their careers in New England are Boston's Denis Leary and Conan O'Brien. Check out ImprovBoston (40 Prospect Street, Cambridge; tel: 617-576-1253; www.improvboston. com) and Comedy Connection at the Wilbur Theatre *(see p.121)* in Boston, and Portland's Custom House Wharf (tel: 207-774-5554; www. mainecomedy.com).

(see p.121)

City Stage & Symphony Hall

1 Columbus Center, Springfield; tel: 413-788-7033; www.symphony hall.com

The 2,611-seat Symphony Hall hosts Broadway-style theatre and classical concerts, while the Blake Theatre stages musicals, drama, and comedy.

The Iron Horse Music Hall

20 Center Street, Northampton; tel: 413-586-8686; www.iheg.com

One of several live music and club venues run by the Iron Horse Group.

Jacob's Pillow Dance

George Carter Road (Route 20), Becket; tel: 413-243-0745; www.jacobspillow.org

An international dance center, which presents ballet and modern works and holds a renowned summer festival.

Shakespeare and Company

70 Kemble Street, Lenox; tel: 413-637-3353; www.shakespeare.org

This venue's summer drama season showcases the Bard's works as well as contemporary playwrights.

Mirabar

35 Richmond Street; tel: 401-331-6761; www.mirabar.com

A gay bar with a variety of theme nights, including retro and karaoke.

Red Fez

49 Peck Street; tel: 401-272-1212

Dark lighting, red walls, animal heads, and an interesting student crowd are features of this hip little restaurant/bar.

Temple Downtown

120 Francis Street; tel: 401-919-5050; www.temple-downtown.com

The city's original Masonic lodge has morphed into a sleek restaurant and cocktail lounge decorated with arty graffiti.

Newport Blues Café

286 Thames Street; tel: 401-841-5510; www.newportblues.com

Newport's best blues venue.

Bar

254 Crown Street, New Haven; tel: 203-495-1111; www.barnightclub.com

An attractive brew pub and club, where you can wash down pizza with the beers, play pool, or dance to the DJ's mix.

Goodspeed Opera House

Route 82, East Haddam; tel: 860-873-8668; www.goodspeed.org

This magnificent opera house presents plays and musicals (Apr–Dec).

Yale Repertory Theatre

Chapel and York streets, New Haven; tel: 203-432-1234; www.yalerep.org

The Yale Rep puts on quality classic and première performances.

The Green Mountains (VT)

Weston Playhouse

Village Green, Weston; tel: 802-824-5288; www.westonplayhouse.org
The Weston puts on Broadway material from June to early September. *See also p.74.*

Burlington (VT)

Flynn Theatre for the Performing Arts

153 Main Street; tel: 802-652-4500; www.flynncenter.org
A restored Art Deco building hosting the Vermont Symphony, drama, and big-name performers.

Nectar's

188 Main Street; tel: 802-658-4771; www.liveatnectars.com
This long-running music bar and restaurant showcases hot local groups, several of whom have gone on to international fame.

Portsmouth (NH)

The Press Room

77 Daniel Street; tel: 603-431-5186; www.pressroomnh.com
Live blues, jazz, folk, R&B, and Latin jazz are performed here seven nights a week.

Seacoast Repertory Theatre

125 Bow Street; tel: 603-433-4793; www.seacoastrep.org
The Seacoast stages year-round drama and musicals.

Portland and Midcoast Maine

Gritty McDuff's

396 Fore Street, Portland; tel: 207-772-2739; www.grittys.com
Portland's original brew pub serves its own fine ales with both typical British pub fare and local seafood dishes.

Portland Center for the Performing Arts

25A Forest Avenue, Portland; tel: 503-248-4335; www.pcpa.com
Theater, dance and music, year-round.

Waterworks

7 Lindsey Street, off Main Street, Rockland; tel: 207-596-2753; www.waterworksrockland.com
A good spot for a Maine microbrew and a bar meal or snack.

The White Heart

551 Congress Street, Portland; tel: 207-828-1900; www.thewhite heart.com
A stylish bar and cocktail lounge where there's dancing nightly (no cover charge) and $2 Bloody Marys with brunch on Sundays.

Down East Maine

Carmen Verandah

119 Main Street, Bar Harbor; tel: 208-288-2886; www.carmenverandah.com
A place to wind down over cocktails and dancing after a day exploring Acadia National Park.

Casinos

Connecticut is home to a couple of giant Vegas-style casinos on Native American reservations land. They offer a range of big-name entertainment to draw customers in for the gambling. Foxwoods (tel: 860-396-6572; www.foxwoods. com) is the world's largest casino, and there's also Mohegan Sun (tel: 888-226-7711; www. mohegansun.com).

CREDITS

Insight Step by Step New England
Written by: Simon Richmond and
Bill and Kay Scheller
Series Editor: Clare Peel
Senior Commissioning Editor: Alex Knights
Cartography Editors: Zoë Goodwin
and James Macdonald
Map Production: Stephen Ramsay
Picture Manager: Steven Lawrence
Art Editor: Ian Spick
Deputy Art Editor: Richard Cooke
Photography: Kindra Clineff 2-1, 2-4, 2-6,
6BL, 7TR, 8-1, 8-4, 8-6, 13TR, 15T, 16T,
18TL, 19B, 20/21T, 23B, 26-3, 26-4, 56/57T,
58/59T, 59TR, 60/61T, 60TL, 62T, 63T, 66C,
68TL, 69TR, 70T, 71T, 77TR, 78/79T, 82T,
86/87T, 87TR, 90/91T, 90TL, 91TR, 93T,
98TL, 98–9T, 104T, 123T; Fotolia 6BR, 72/73T,
72TL; iStockphoto.com 4-2, 4-3, 7BR, 8/9,
10T, 11T, 12TL, 25T, 26-2, 64TL, 65TR,
68/69T, 73TR, 76/77T, 76TL, 78TL, 80T,
86TL, 88T, 92T; Leonardo 107T, 108T, 111TR;
Abe Nowitz/Apa 4-4, 8-5, 15B, 16B, 20TL, 26-
1, 26-6, 28T, 29T, 30T, 34B, 34T, 35T, 37B, 38T,
39T, 40/41T, 41TR, 46/47T, 46B, 46C, 46TL,
50T, 52T, 56TL, 94-1, 103T, 116TL; Daniella
Nowitz/Apa 28C, 31T, 32TL, 94-2, 96TL,
102T, 105T; Richard Nowitz/Apa 2-5, 2/3, 4-1,
4-5, 6TR, 7BL, 7CR, 7TL, 8-3, 11B, 14B, 14T,
17T, 18/19T, 19TR, 23T, 24T, 26/27, 30B,
32/33, 33TR, 36T, 38CB, 38CT, 40TL, 42B,
42T, 43T, 44T, 45T, 47TR, 48T, 49T, 51B, 51C,
51T, 52B, 53T, 54/55T, 57TR, 94/95, 96/97T,
97TR, 99TR, 100T, 101T, 117TR, 120TL;
Portland Museum of Art 2-2, 89T

Front cover: main image: 4Corners Images;
bottom left: iStockphoto; bottom right:
Richard Nowitz/Apa.

Printed by: Insight Print Services (Pte) Ltd,
38 Joo Koon Road, Singapore 628990

CONTACTING THE EDITORS

We would appreciate it if readers would alert us
to errors or outdated information by writing to
us at insight@apaguide.co.uk or APA Publications,
PO Box 7910, London SE1 1WE, UK.

www.insightguides.com

DISTRIBUTION

Worldwide
APA Publications GmbH & Co. Verlag KG
(Singapore branch)
38 Joo Koon Road
Singapore 628990
Tel: (65) 6865 1600
E-mail: apasin@singnet.com.sg

UK and Ireland
GeoCenter International Ltd
Meridian House, Churchill Way West
Basingstoke, Hampshire, RG21 6YR
Tel: (44) 01256 817 987
E-mail: sales@geocenter.co.uk

United States
Langenscheidt Publishers, Inc.
36–36 33rd Street, 4th Floor
Long Island City, NY 11106
Tel: (1) 718 784 0055
E-mail: orders@langenscheidt.com

Australia
Universal Publishers
1 Waterloo Road, Macquarie Park, NSW 2113
Tel: (61) 2 9857 3700
E-mail: sales@universalpublishers.com.au

New Zealand
Hema Maps New Zealand Ltd (HNZ)
Unit 2, 10 Cryers Road
East Tamaki, Auckland 2013
Tel: (64) 9 273 6459
E-mail: sales.hema@clear.net.nz

INDEX